The Day of the Jackal

Adapted by Dorothy Welchman
from *The Day of the Jackal*
by Frederick Forsyth

Hutchinson
London Melbourne Sydney Auckland Johannesburg

Hutchinson & Co. (Publishers) Ltd

Brookmount House, 62–65 Chandos Place
Covent Garden, London, WC2N 4NW

Hutchinson Publishing Group (Australia) Pty Ltd
16–22 Church Street, Hawthorn, Melbourne, Victoria 3122

Hutchinson Group (NZ) Ltd
32–34 View Road, PO Box 40-086, Glenfield, Auckland 10

Hutchinson Group (SA) (Pty) Ltd
PO Box 337, Bergvlei 2012, South Africa

Original novel first published by Hutchinson 1971
© Frederick Forsyth 1971

This adaptation first published 1978
Reprinted 1979, 1980, 1982, 1985
© This adaptation Dorothy Welchman 1978

Set in Intertype Baskerville

Printed and bound in Great Britain by
Anchor Brendon Ltd, Tiptree, Essex

ISBN 0 09 133551 5

Contents

Part Three   **The Kill**

Part One
The Plot

1 Death in the morning

It is cold at six-forty in the morning. It seems even colder when a man is about to be shot by firing squad. At that hour on 11 March 1963 a French Air Force colonel stood with his hands tied behind a post. 'Take aim,' the squad leader shouted. There was a crash of rifle fire and it was all over.

The dead man had led a gang of French Secret Army killers in a plot to kill the President of France. The death of the colonel was meant to put an end to any more plots to kill the President. Instead it was a new beginning.

The Secret Army, known as the OAS, hated the President. They had sworn to get rid of him and his Government. They believed that he had betrayed France and the French living in Algeria. Three million French people lived there. But some of the Algerians wanted to get the French out of their country. French soldiers were sent out to Algeria to fight for the French people living there. The war went on for several years. In 1959 President de Gaulle came to power as the man who would finish the war and keep Algeria part of France. But two years later he gave up and called the French Army back to France. Some of them refused to go. They felt he had betrayed them. They formed a secret army. The OAS leaders dared not return to France. Their names were known to the President and his Government. They were forced to stay abroad.

The chief of the OAS was Colonel Marc Rodin. He was in Austria. Later that same morning he was listening to the radio news in a small hotel. He heard the report of the shooting by firing squad of one of his men.

Rodin said, 'Bastards.' He said it with hate and followed it with a string of foul words that showed how much he hated the French President, the Government and the Action Service. It was the Action Service that had caught and shot the man.

The Action Service was at the head of the anti-OAS war. It was part of the French Secret Service and was made up of hundreds of tough men. They were trained to be very fit and were experts in fighting with small arms, karate and judo. They had orders to kill if need be and to use kidnapping, torture and arson. The OAS hated them even more than they hated the police.

Marc Rodin was tall and thin and his face showed the hatred inside him. He had been an officer in the French Army fighting in Algeria. He was one of the rebels who had formed the OAS.

Now on the morning of 11 March he sat at the window of his hotel room chain-smoking. He was a man with a lot of cunning and common sense and had a good brain. He was using all these now on the problem of killing the French President.

He was no fool. He knew the job would not be easy. Other plots had failed. In fact, the failure of the latest plot would make things even harder. There would be more guards than ever round the President now. The problem was to find a man or a plan unusual enough to get through these guards.

For two hours he thought about the problem. Things had changed since the last plot. The French police had raided house after house. They had found stores of weapons. Action Service spies were now inside the ranks of the OAS. There were no lengths to which the Action Service would not go to get at the leaders of the OAS and to question them. The OAS leaders were on the run. There had been a rush for false papers and tickets to other countries.

Watching this, the lower ranks were losing heart. Men inside France had been ready to help; to shelter wanted men; to carry arms; to pass messages. Now they were hanging up the phone with muttered excuses. To find men willing to help now would be hard indeed. The faces of those who *were* willing were well known to the French police and to several million ordinary people besides. Any new plan set up at this stage would be 'blown' at once if it meant getting OAS members together to plan it.

2 An outside chance

The answer came to Rodin just before noon. If he could find a man who was not known. . . . He ran through the list of men he knew would not stop at killing a president. Every one had a file as thick as the Bible at police HQ. Why else would he, Marc Rodin, be hiding in a hotel in a little Austrian village? If only such a man could be found.

Rodin put on his coat and went downstairs. Turning left, he went towards the post office. He sent a number of short telegrams to his OAS friends who were living in Germany, Austria, Italy and Spain. The message was that he would not be around for a few weeks as he was busy on a job.

By mid-afternoon he was gone, bags packed, his hotel bill paid. He was off to find a man, or at least a kind of man, he did not even know existed.

Ninety days later Rodin's search was over. He arrived back in Austria and booked in to a small hotel in Vienna. From the main post office he sent off two telegrams. They were to his two chief officers, telling them to come at once to an important meeting in Vienna.

Within twenty-four hours the men had arrived. René Montclair came by hired car from another part of the country; André Casson flew in from Rome. Both had travelled under false names as they were on the wanted lists.

As host, Rodin seated the other two in the bedroom's two easy chairs. He took the upright chair behind the plain table for himself. Rodin poured them both a brandy and as they drank he looked at them keenly over his own glass.

René Montclair was short and stocky. Like Rodin he had been an officer in the Army. He had been in the pay branch. By the spring of 1963 he was in charge of the OAS funds. André Casson was small and neat. He had been a bank manager in Algeria. Now he ran the OAS underground in France. Both men were, like Rodin, very tough, even among the OAS.

Rodin began his briefing. He listed the defeats the OAS had had at the hands of the Action Service over the past few months.

'We simply must face facts,' he said. 'The Action Service have now got right inside our movement and know of the plans of even our highest councils. They know who our men are. As I see it, there is only one way to kill the President. We must get an outsider to do it.'

Montclair and Casson looked up quickly.

'What kind of outsider?' Casson asked.

'He would have to be from outside France,' Rodin said. 'He would not be known to any policeman in France, nor would he be on any file. He would do the job and then vanish back to his own country. The important thing is that he would be able to get in to France, without being spotted or suspected. To get the man out again would be no problem. After we had taken power from the President's men, we would free him. An outsider would be able to get in, and that is something which, at the moment, not one of us can do.'

Montclair let out a low whistle.

'A hired killer.'

'Exactly,' Rodin said. 'And such a man would only work for money, a lot of money.'

'But how do we know we can find such a man?' asked Casson.

Rodin held up his hand.

'First things first, gentlemen. What I wish to know first is if you agree to the idea.'

Montclair and Casson nodded slowly.

'Good.' Rodin sat back in his chair. 'That's the first point then. The second is about silence. There are now very few people who we can really trust. The whole point of the idea is that it should be kept secret. The fewer who know about it the better. I have called you two here because I know you can be trusted and that you can keep your mouths shut. Montclair. as paymaster, you will have to take over the job of paying the killer. Casson, you will be able to get hold of a small group of loyal men inside France, in case the killer needs their help. But I see no reason why the idea should go further than the three of us. Do you agree?'

Again Montclair and Casson nodded.

Rodin looked at them both and smiled. 'Good,' he said. 'Now let us get down to details. I have been searching for the man we want. Such men are hard to find, of course. The results can be found in these.'

He held up three folders that had been lying on his desk.

'I think it would be best if you look through the folders, then we can talk about who we think would be best. I have already chosen the one I think is right for the job.'

When Montclair and Casson had read through all three files Rodin took them and put them back on the desk.

'For the moment,' he said, 'let us call them simply the German, the South African and the Englishman. Casson, what do you think?'

Casson said, 'For me there is no problem. The Englishman is about a mile ahead.'

'Montclair?' Rodin asked.

Montclair said, 'I agree. The German is a bit old for this kind of thing now. The South African does not seem to be in quite the right class for a killing of this sort. Besides, the Englishman speaks very good French.'

Rodin nodded slowly. 'I did not think there would be much of a problem.'

Casson said, 'Are you sure about this Englishman? Has he really done all these jobs?'

'I was surprised myself,' Rodin agreed. 'So I spent extra time on this one. There is no complete proof. If there were it would be a bad sign. It would mean that he was a wanted man. As it is there is nothing against him, only stories. For this job he is perfect in all ways but one.'

'What's that?' asked Montclair quickly.

'Simple,' Rodin said. 'He will not be cheap. A man like him can ask a lot of money. How are the funds, Montclair?'

'Not too good,' Montclair said. 'Very little money is coming in. Something must be done or we shall be finished for lack of funds. You can't run this sort of thing on love and kisses.'

Rodin nodded grimly. 'I thought so. We have to raise some money from somewhere. But first we must find out how much we are going to need.'

'So,' Casson said smoothly, 'the next step is to get in touch with the Englishman and ask him if he will do the job and for how much.'

'Yes, well, are we all agreed on that?' Rodin asked.

Both the others nodded. Rodin looked at his watch.

'It is now just after one o'clock. I have a contact in London who can get in touch with this man. If he is willing to fly to Vienna tonight, on the evening plane, we could meet him here after dinner. I have booked you into rooms next door to each other down the corridor.'

Rodin called in his bodyguard who had been outside the door. He was a giant of a man called Viktor. He turned to the other two and said, 'I have to telephone from the main post office. I shall take Viktor with me. While we are gone would you both stay together in one room with the door locked. My signal will be three knocks, a pause, then two more.'

3   Enter the Englishman

The BEA plane from London to Vienna reached the airport at nightfall. Near the tail of the plane sat a blond Englishman. From his seat near the window he watched the landing lights A message had come through to him a few hours before – to fly to Vienna and report to a certain hotel.

He walked out of the airport building and got a taxi. Forty minutes later the taxi stopped outside the hotel. Inside, he took the stairs two at a time without seeming to hurry. He knew he was expected in room 64. At the top he stopped and looked down the only corridor. At the far end was room 68. He counted back down the corridor to what must be 64, although the numbers were not in view. Between himself and the door of 64 was twenty feet of corridor. On the right were two other doors before room 64 and on the left, a small alcove partly covered with red velvet curtains.

He looked at the alcove carefully. From underneath the curtain the toe of a black shoe could just be seen. He turned and went back down to the entrance hall.

'Get me room 64, please,' he said to the clerk. The clerk looked him in the face for a second and then went over to a small switchboard. He picked up the desk phone and passed it over to the blond man.

'If that gorilla is not out of the alcove in fifteen seconds I am going back home,' he said and put the phone down. Then he walked back up the stairs.

At the top he watched the door of 64 open and Rodin came out. He stared down the corridor for a moment, then called softly, 'Viktor.' From the alcove the great giant of a man appeared and stood looking from Rodin to the blond man.

Rodin said, 'It's all right. He is expected.' Viktor frowned. The Englishman started to walk towards Rodin.

Rodin showed him into the bedroom. Montclair and Casson looked at the visitor keenly. The Englishman sat down and stared back at them. Rodin closed the door and took his seat behind the desk.

For a few seconds he stared at the man from London. What he saw pleased him, and he was an expert in men. The visitor was about six feet tall, in his early thirties, with a lean, athletic build. He looked fit and his face was tanned. His hands lay quietly along the arms of the chair. To Rodin he looked like a man who was in control of himself. But the eyes troubled Rodin. They were completely cold eyes that showed no feelings.

Rodin began, 'We know who you are; I had better tell you who I am. I am Colonel Marc Rodin. . . .'

'I know,' said the Englishman. 'You are chief of the OAS.' He turned to the other two. 'You are René Montclair, the paymaster, and you are André Casson, head of the underground in Paris.'

'You seem to know a lot already,' Casson said.

'Gentlemen,' the Englishman said, 'let us be frank. I know what you are and you know what I am. We both have unusual jobs. You are hunted while I am free to go where I want. I work for money, you work for ideals. You have been asking questions about me. Of course, I heard about it. Two days in the British Museum among the French newspaper files was enough to tell me about the OAS. So your message this afternoon was hardly a surprise. What I would like to know is what you want.'

Rodin said, 'You have read the files. We believe that the President of France has betrayed his country. We believe that France can only be given back to Frenchmen if he first dies. Our efforts at killing him have so far always gone wrong. We are thinking of getting a hired killer to do the job. But we do not want to waste our money. The first thing we would like to know is if it is possible.'

The last remark brought some interest to the cold eyes of the Englishman. He said, 'There is no man in the world who is safe from a bullet. But in this case the job would be a very hard one. More so than with most other men.'

'Why more than others?' Montclair asked.

'Because, gentlemen, not only have your own efforts to kill the President failed, they have messed things up for everyone else. The President will be guarded now more closely than ever.'

Rodin began to say, 'If we *do* hire a killer to do this job. . . .'

'You must hire a killer,' cut in the Englishman. 'You three men did not call me here for a cosy chat. You have called me here because you know that there are French Secret Service spies inside the OAS. So nothing that you decide stays a secret for very long. Also the face of every one of you is printed on the memory of every policeman in France. You need an outsider. The only question is who, and for how much. Now, gentlemen, I think you have had long enough to look at the goods, don't you?'

4 How much?

Rodin looked sideways at Montclair and Casson. They both nodded. The Englishman showed no interest and looked out of the window.

At last Rodin asked, 'Will you kill the President of France?'

The voice was quiet but the question filled the room. The Englishman looked at him and the eyes were cold and blank.

'Yes, but it will cost a lot of money,' he said.

'How much?' asked Montclair.

'You understand that this is a one-off job. The man who does it will never work again. The chances of not getting caught are slim. The money must be enough to be able to live well for the rest of my life.'

'When we have France,' said Casson, 'we shall have plenty of money.'

'I want cash,' said the Englishman. 'Half now and half when the job is done.'

'How much?' Rodin asked.

'Half a million dollars.'

'Half a million dollars?' shouted Montclair, getting up from his seat. 'Are you crazy?'

'No,' said the Englishman calmly. 'But I am the best and so the dearest. Considering you expect to get France itself, you hold your country very cheap.'

Rodin said, 'I take your point. The trouble is we do not have half a million dollars in cash.'

'I know that,' said the Englishman. 'If you want the job done you will have to find that much from somewhere. I do not need the job, you understand. I have enough to live well for some years. But I like the idea of having enough to retire on. I am willing to take some very high risks for that. If you cannot get hold of the money you must go back to making your own plots and seeing them fail one by one.'

He got up. Rodin stood up, too. 'Sit down, sir,' Rodin said. 'We shall get the money.' They both sat down.

'Good,' said the Englishman. 'Now, how many people know of this plan to get an outsider to do the job?'

'Just the three of us in this room,' Rodin told him.

'Then it must stay that way,' said the Englishman. 'You three should stay somewhere safe, under heavy guard, until the job is done. Agreed?'

'Agreed,' said Rodin. 'Anything else?'

'The planning will be mine. I shall tell no one the details, not even you. You will hear nothing from me again. I shall give you the name of my Swiss bank. When they tell me that the first half of the money is paid in, I shall move as soon as I am ready. I will not be rushed and I must do it in my own way. Agreed?'

'Agreed,' Rodin said. 'But our undercover men in France could give you a lot of help and information. Some of them are in high places.'

The Englishman thought about this for a moment. 'All right.

When you are ready send me a single phone number by post – if possible a Paris number. Then I can ring direct from anywhere in France. I will not tell anyone where I am. I will just ring that number for the latest on the President's moves. But the man on the end of that phone must not know what I am doing in France. The less he knows the better.'

Rodin said, 'There is one last point. Your code name. Do you have any ideas?'

The Englishman was silent for a moment. Then he said, 'Since we have been speaking of hunting, what about "the Jackal". Will that do?'

Rodin nodded, 'Yes, that will do fine.'

He showed the Englishman to the door and opened it. Viktor came out from his alcove. Rodin smiled and held out his hand to the killer.

'We will be in touch in the agreed manner as soon as we can. Good-bye, Mr Jackal.'

Viktor watched the visitor go as quietly as he had come. The Englishman spent the night at the airport hotel and caught the first plane back to London the next morning.

Inside the hotel Rodin faced the music from Casson and Montclair.

'Half a million dollars,' Montclair kept saying. 'How on earth do we get half a million dollars?'

'We may have to rob a few banks,' Rodin said.

5   The Jackal does his homework

During the second half of June and all of July 1963 France was rocked by an outbreak of crime. There had never been anything like it before or since. Banks were held up with pistols and sawn-off shotguns nearly every day. There were smash-and-grab raids at jewellers' shops. Two bank clerks were shot in different towns as they tried to stop the robbers. By the end of July the problem was so big that anti-riot squads were called in. For the first time, they were armed with submachine-guns. People going into banks had to pass one or two armed guards in the doorway.

It did not take long for the French police to catch on that the OAS was behind the crimes. They also knew that it meant the OAS needed money in a hurry. But they did not know why. By the end of July well over two million new francs (or 400 000 dollars) had been stolen.

It was near the end of June that the chief of police in Paris had a report from police HQ in Rome. It said that the three top men of the OAS, Rodin, Montclair and Casson were living together on the top floor of a hotel in Rome. The three had, at great cost, taken the whole of the top floor for themselves, and the floor below for their bodyguards. They were being guarded night and day by no fewer than eight guards, and were not going out at all. It was thought that they were making quite sure that they would not be kidnapped and made to talk, as other OAS men had been in the past. The report was filed away. It was only much later that the chief of police found out why the three OAS men were being so careful.

In London the Jackal spent the last two weeks of June and the first two weeks of July making careful plans. He had set himself to read just about every word written about the President of France, Charles de Gaulle. He read until the small hours each morning in his flat. He built up a complete picture of the man in his mind. Much of what he read was of no real use. But every now and then something about the President's ways would come to light. He wrote these down in a small notebook. But this still did not solve the main problem – when, where and how should the 'hit' take place? In the end he went down to the Reading Room of the British Museum. He signed the form they gave him with a false name. Then he started to work his way through the back copies of the French daily newspapers. He found out from them on just what day, come illness or bad weather, the President would be sure to be seen in public. From that point on, he stopped reading and started to plan the details.

It took him long hours of thought, lying on his back in his flat and smoking his usual king-size filters. He threw out at least a dozen ideas before he hit on the one that was good enough. He now knew not only when and where, but how.

The Jackal knew that not only was General de Gaulle the President of France, he was also the most closely guarded man in the Western world. He knew that he was up against the best bodyguards in the world, and that they had already had warnings about plots to kill the man they guarded. On the other hand, no one knew about *him*. His name was on no police files. He also knew from his reading that the President was a proud and stubborn man. On the chosen day the President would come out into the open for a few moments, no matter how high the risks to himself.

6 Stolen papers

The airliner from Denmark came to land in front of the airport buildings in London. The steps were wheeled out and the passengers started to file out. On the visitor's terrace the blond man took off his dark glasses and looked through a pair of field-glasses. It was the sixth time that morning that he had watched a plane come in. But the terrace was crowded and no one took any notice of him.

As the last passenger came down the steps the blond man watched him keenly. The passenger from Denmark was a parson in a dark grey suit with a dog collar. He looked to be in his late forties. He was a tall man with wide shoulders and he looked very fit. He was about the same build as the Jackal.

As the passengers filed into customs, the Jackal went down into the main hall. When the parson came out of the hall to get on the BEA bus the Jackal was a few paces behind him. They drove into London on the same bus. When the bus got to Cromwell Road the parson went towards the taxi rank. The Jackal walked quickly across the bus-park to where he had left his sports car. He got in and started up, bringing the car to a halt where he could watch the long line of waiting taxis. The parson got into the third taxi. The sports car followed it.

The taxi dropped the parson at a small hotel in Half Moon Street. The sports car shot past and stopped further up the street. Within five minutes the Jackal was walking into the hotel. He had to wait another twenty minutes before the parson came down. The girl at the desk took his room key and hung it up. The key swung for a few seconds on its hook. The Jackal saw that the key number was 47. A few minutes later, when the girl left the desk for a moment, the Jackal slipped quietly up the stairs.

With a strip of mica and a small knife he sprang the lock on the door of room 47. The parson had left his passport on the bed-side table. There was also a wallet with some money in it. The Jackal was out of the hotel in a matter of minutes. He left the wallet behind in the hope that it would make the parson think there had been no theft. And that is what did happen. Later in the afternoon the parson reported to the Danish Consul that he had lost his passport. They gave him a form to get him back to Denmark at the end of his two-week stay in London. The Consul clerk filed the report of the loss of a passport in the name of Pastor Per Jensen and thought no more about it. The date was 14 July.

Two days later an American student lost his passport. He had flown from New York. At the airport he put his hand-grip down for a moment while he tried to get a porter. Three seconds later it was gone. The report of the loss went, in the end, to the London police. The report was filed, but as weeks passed and neither the bag nor the passport were found, no more was thought about it.

The student, who was called Marty Schulberg, went to his Consul and was given forms to get him back to America at the end of his stay. In spite of the differences in their ages, the two who had lost their passports had some things in common. Both were about six feet tall, had wide shoulders and were slim. Both had blue eyes. They both looked quite like the Englishman who had robbed them. On the other hand, the parson was forty-eight years old, with grey hair and gold-rimmed glasses for reading. Marty Schulberg was twenty-five with chestnut brown hair and heavy-rimmed glasses.

These were the faces the Jackal looked at keenly in the passports on his desk at the flat. Then he made several trips to shops – a man's clothing shop, a shop that sold theatre clothes and several others. He did not buy more than one thing at any one shop. He came back with a pair of black sneakers, a T-shirt, white slacks and a blue windcheater with red and white cuffs. All these were made in New York. He also bought a parson's white shirt, dog collar and black bib front. From these he cut out the makers' labels. As well as a pair of glasses with gold rims, he bought another pair with heavy black frames and a set of blue-tinted contact lenses. His last trip of the day was to a shop selling men's wigs. Here he bought some stuff for tinting hair grey and some more for tinting it chestnut brown. He was also told how to use the tint to get the best results in a short time.

7 To the graveyard

The next day, 18 July, there was a short notice in the newspaper. It said that in Paris the deputy chief of the Crime Squad had died. His place was to be taken by Claude Lebel of the

Murder Squad. The Jackal read this notice but thought nothing of it.

His thoughts were on passports. It is quite easy to get yourself a false British passport. First the Jackal went out in his car looking at graveyards in small villages. In the third one he visited he found what he was looking for. It was the grave-stone of Alexander Duggan, who had died at the age of two and a half in 1931. Had he lived, the child would by now have been about as old as the Jackal. The Jackal called at the vicar's house. The old vicar was kind and helpful. He showed the Jackal the parish record books. They showed that both the Duggan parents had died over the past seven years. The Jackal turned over the pages in the record books. Under the births for 1929 he found the entry he was looking for: Alexander James Duggan, born 3 April 1929.

He thanked the vicar and left. Back in London he went to the Register of Births, Marriages and Deaths. A search of the records showed that the child had died on 8 November 1931. For a few shillings he was able to buy a copy of both the birth and death certificates. He also bought a toy printing set from a toy shop and got a passport application form from a post office.

He went back to his flat and filled in the form. He put down his own height, colour of hair and eyes. For job he wrote 'businessman'. But he gave his name as 'Alexander James Duggan' and the date and place of birth of the dead child. He forged the name of the vicar he had met that morning. He had seen the vicar's full name on a board outside the church. With the toy printing set he made up a stamp reading 'St Mark's Parish Church' and the address of the church. He used this underneath the vicar's name. He sent the form off to the passport office with a copy of the birth certificate and a postal order for £1. He burned the death certificate.

The new passport came by post four days later. Soon after, he locked the flat and drove to London Airport. He bought a ticket with cash so as not to have to sign a cheque. Then he got on a plane to Denmark. His visit there was short and to the point. He bought a grey suit, a pair of black walking shoes, some socks, underwear and three white shirts. In the case of the shirts the idea was simply to get hold of the Danish labels in them. He would sew them on to the parson's shirt, dog collar and bib front that he had bought in London.

He caught the evening plane, not back to London, but to Brussels. He had to meet someone who lived there.

8 Guns for sale

On the morning of 21 July 1963, Paul Goossens waited for his English visitor. Goossens ran a thriving business in black market arms. He sold them to half the underworld in Western Europe. Although he had a fine war record, he also had had a long spell in prison for stealing money from the firm he worked for. His wife left him, taking the children with her. His career was over, but he had been the firm's top expert in making weapons of all kinds, from small pistols to heavy machine guns.

Goossens showed the Englishman into his little office at noon. When the Jackal had taken a seat, Goossens said, 'What can I do for you, sir?'

The Jackal said, 'I have a job on hand for which I shall need a special kind of rifle.'

'What had you in mind?' Goossens asked.

'It is a question of finding the right gun for the job,' the Jackal said. 'It must be quite slim. It must be a bolt-action rifle. On the other hand, it cannot have a bolt with a handle that sticks out to the side. The bolt must slide straight back to the shoulder. And the trigger must be one that can be fixed on just before firing.'

25

'Why?' Goossens asked.

'Because the whole thing must slide into a tube for carrying.'

Goossens beamed with pleasure, 'A one-off job. A gun that will be tailor-made for one man and one job.'

'Exactly,' the Jackal said. 'A job that will never be done again.'

'You have come to the right man,' Goossens said. 'I am glad that you came.'

'So am I,' the Jackal said. 'The gun must also be light and have a short barrel. . . .'

'Over what range will you have to fire?' Goossens asked.

'That is still not certain, but probably not more than one hundred and thirty metres.'

Goossens said, 'Will you go for a head or a chest shot?'

'It will probably have to be head. I may get a shot at the chest, but the head is a better bet.'

'Sure to kill if you get a good hit,' Goossens agreed. 'But the chest is more likely to get a good hit. I take it from what you say that there could be someone passing in the way?'

'Yes, there may be,' the Jackal told him.

'Will you get the chance of a second shot?'

'I might if I use a silencer,' the Jackal said. 'And a silencer would help me to get away. There must be several clear minutes before anyone nearby even guesses where the bullet has come from.'

Goossens nodded. 'Explosive bullets would be best,' he said. 'You are more likely to kill with one shot. Are there any more points?'

'Yes. For firing, it must have a frame stock like a Sten gun. Each of the three parts must unscrew into three separate rods. It must also have a telescopic sight.'

Goossens thought for a moment.

'Well, can you do it?' the Jackal asked.

Goossens smiled. 'It is quite a job. But yes, I can do it. I have never failed yet. Really what you have described is a gun that can be taken past certain check-points without being seen. A hunter needs a hunting rifle and that is what you shall have.

It will be light and slim, but with explosive bullets, just the thing for bigger game. I will fit a frame-stock of three separate steel rods. The screw-in trigger is no problem. I can shorten the barrel by eight inches. I shall make the silencer myself. Now, sir, you said it must have some sort of tubes for carrying the parts of the broken-down gun. What had you in mind?'

The Jackal went over to the desk. He got a pencil out of his pocket and drew on the desk pad for a few seconds.

'Do you see what this is?' he asked turning the pad back to the gunsmith.

'Of course,' Goossens said, after looking at the well-drawn sketch. His eyes were wide with surprise. 'Sir, you are a genius. So simple, yet no one would guess.'

The Jackal said, 'Right. Well now, the whole thing is made up of hollow metal tubes which screw together. This one,' he said, tapping the sketch with his pencil, 'will have one of the struts of the rifle stock in it. This one has the other strut. The shoulder rest is this . . . here. This one is the widest tube and it will hold the breech and barrel of the rifle. These two parts contain the telescopic sight and the silencer. The bullets should go into this little stump here.'

'Good,' Goossens said. 'It shall be done.'

The Jackal said, 'I shall need the gun in about two weeks.'

'Come back on 1 August,' Goossens said. 'Then we can talk over any last-minute problems. Then you can have the finished gun on 4 August.'

'Now, have you any idea how much it will cost?' the Jackal asked him.

Goossens thought for a while. 'It will be dear. It means a lot of work. I must ask a fee of one thousand pounds. This will not just be a rifle, it will be a work of art. Then, on top, there will be the price of the parts, say another two hundred pounds.'

'Done,' said the Englishman. He put his hand into his breast pocket and brought out a bundle of fivers. 'I will give you five hundred pounds now and the other seven hundred when I come back. Does that suit you?'

27

'It is a pleasure to deal with you, sir,' the gunsmith said. He put the notes quickly into his pocket.

'There is something else,' the Jackal said. 'You will not try to find out who I am or who I am working for. If you do, I shall hear about it. And if that happens, you will die. Is that clear?'

'Sir,' the gunsmith said quietly, 'I do not want to know anything about you. The gun will have no serial number. It is important to me that nothing you do should ever come back on me. Good-bye, sir.'

9   Forgery

The Jackal walked away into the bright sunshine. Two streets away he got a taxi. The taxi took him to a bar where he had fixed a meeting with a forger.

The Jackal found his man already sitting in a corner of the bar. When he had made himself known, the Jackal got out his driving licence. It was in his own name and it had some months still to run.

He told the forger, 'This belonged to a man who is now dead. As I am banned from driving in Britain, I need a new front page in my own name, Duggan.' He put the passport in the name of Duggan in front of the forger. The man looked at the passport and saw that it was a very new one. He looked keenly at the Jackal. Then he looked at the driving licence. After a few moments he looked up. 'This is no great problem. Was that all you wanted?'

'No, there are two other papers,' the Jackal told him.

'Ah. I thought it was odd that you should contact me for such a simple job. There must be men in your own London who could do this. What are the other papers?'

The Jackal told him what he wanted down to the very last detail. The man thought for a moment. 'That is not so easy. The French identity card is not so bad. There are plenty of those about to copy from. But the other one is harder. I do not think I have ever seen one.'

He paused while the Jackal called to a passing waiter to fill up their drinks. When the waiter had gone he went on.

'And then the photograph. That will not be easy. You say there must be a change in age and hair colour. Most people ask for false papers with their own photograph but a different name. But to make up a photograph which does not even look like you as you are now – that makes things tricky.'

The forger thought for a while, staring at the photo in the passport. He wrote down the name Alexander Duggan on a piece of paper. Then he closed the passport and handed it back to the Jackal. He put the piece of paper and the driving licence into his pocket.

'All right,' he said. 'It can be done. I may have to get a mate who is a pickpocket to get the second of these cards you need.'

'How much is your fee?' the Jackal asked.

The forger said, 'One hundred and fifty pounds.'

'All right. I will give you one hundred pounds now, and the rest when the papers are ready.'

The forger nodded. 'Then we had better get the photos done. I have my own studio.'

They took a taxi to a small flat. It was more than a mile away. The forger led the way down the steps and unlocked the front door. Inside was a dirty old studio. In one corner was a large trunk. When the forger unlocked it, the Jackal saw that it was full of cameras, flash bulbs, make-up, glasses and wigs.

The forger worked for half an hour on the Jackal's face. With clever make-up he turned it into the face of an old man with ash-grey skin and dark rings under the eyes. Then he took a grey wig from the trunk and fitted it on the Jackal's head.

The forger took six photos of the Jackal. He went into the

dark room and came out some time later with the prints in his hand. Together they looked at them. Staring up at them was the face of an old man.

'You can copy it easily,' the forger told him. 'The main point is the hair. It must be cut like this, before you use the photo. And it must be tinted grey. You can grow three days' beard stubble. Then shave with a cut-throat razor, but do it badly. Old men tend to cut themselves when shaving. As for the skin, this is important. It must be grey and tired-looking. Can you get hold of some pieces of cordite?'

'Yes, I think so.'

The forger said, 'Two or three small bits of cordite, eaten, make you feel sick within half an hour. They also make the skin turn grey and make the face sweat. We used this trick in the Army to get out of route marches.'

The Jackal said, 'Thank you for all the know-how. Now, do you think you can have the papers ready in time?'

'I think I can do it all by the first few days of August,' the forger said.

The Jackal took off the wig and wiped his face with a towel soaked in spirit. From his pocket he took a bundle of fivers which he handed to the man. As he did so he said, 'There are certain things I wish to make clear. When you have done the job, you will give me all the negs and all the prints. Also the old front page from my driving licence – as well as the new papers. You will also forget my name and the name Duggan. The name on the two cards you are going to make for me can be anything. Just pick a common French name. After handing the papers over you will forget that name, too. You will never speak to anyone of this job again. If you do, you will die. Is that clear?'

'It is understood, sir.'

A few seconds later the Jackal was gone into the night. He walked for five blocks, then took a taxi back to his hotel. He had a bath to get rid of the last traces of make-up.

The next morning he checked out of the hotel and took the train to Paris.

10   Rue de Rennes

The Jackal's train got to Paris just before lunch. He took a taxi to a small hotel. He signed in as Alexander Duggan.

On his first day he bought a street map of Paris. He spent three days going to see places of interest. He might have been any English holiday-maker. In fact he was looking for the perfect spot for the killing. His last visit was to the square at the end of the street called Rue de Rennes. There was something about this square. It was full of memories of the Second World War. The square had been given a new name when the President's men took over. The Jackal looked at the shiny new name-plate which said '*18 June 1940*'. That was the day when the President had told the French over the air that if they had lost a battle, they had not lost the war.

On the south side of the square were the big buildings of a main-line railway station.

Slowly the Jackal looked at the square. It was full of traffic now, as he walked round. He looked through the railings into the court of the big main-line station. It was due to be pulled down that winter. The Jackal turned with his back to the railings and looked down the street called Rue de Rennes. He was sure that this was the place the President of France would visit, one last time, on the chosen day. From the top floor of the corner house on the west side of the Rue de Rennes to the station yard was about 130 metres.

The Jackal walked slowly over to a café and ordered a coffee. He sat outside and stared at the houses across the street. He sat there for three hours. Later, he had lunch at a café on the other side of the street and again he spent a long time staring at the houses on the other side. In the afternoon he walked up and down, looking closer at the buildings he might use for the kill.

The next day he was back again. He sat on a bench under the trees and pretended to be reading a newspaper. In fact, he was looking at the upper floors of the flats. Above five or six floors there were tiled roofs with little attic windows. At one time they must have been servants' rooms. Now they would be flats for poorer people. The roofs and the attic rooms would be watched on the day. But the top floor, just below the attics, would be high enough. If he sat back in the darkness of the room, he would not be seen from the street.

The time of day for the 'hit' would be the middle of the afternoon. So he waited until four o'clock. The sun was still high enough to shine over the station roof into the houses on the east side of the street. So he ruled out the blocks on the east side. That left him with only two possible flats on the west side.

The next day he spotted the caretaker. She was sitting in her doorway. She looked up from her knitting to bid 'good morning' to the people who went in and out of her block. They said, 'Good morning, Bertha.' She seemed to be well liked, a motherly body. The Jackal thought she looked the sort who would have pity on the old and poor.

Just before four o'clock she put her knitting down and went down the road to the baker's. The Jackal got up quietly from his bench. He went into the flats and ran up the stairs rather than use the lift.

On the sixth floor there were two doors into the flats at the front of the block. These would have windows looking down into the Rue de Rennes. He listened for a moment, but there was no sound from either flat. He looked at the strong locks on the doors. He would need keys. Bertha would be sure to have them in her room downstairs. A few seconds later he was running down the stairs. On each landing there was a door to a steel fire-escape. On the first floor he opened this door and looked out. The fire-escape led to an inner yard with a narrow alley leading to the street. He had found his escape route.

He closed the door and ran lightly down the stairs. He had been in the block less than five minutes. The caretaker was back. He could just see her through the glass door of her room.

He turned left up the street. He was looking up and down for a taxi when a policeman on a motorcycle swept into the square. He jerked his machine on to its stand and began to halt the traffic with shrill blasts on his whistle. The traffic had just come to a stand-still when the police sirens were heard. Five hundred yards away, the Jackal saw a motorcade heading towards him.

In the lead were two motorbikes with riders in white helmets. They were followed by two black Citroën DS 19s. In the back of the first one was a tall man in a dark grey suit. The Jackal caught sight of the head and the large nose before the motorcade was gone. It was a face you could not mistake. It was General Charles de Gaulle.

'The next time I see your face,' the Jackal said to himself, 'it will be through a telescopic sight.'

11 Jacqueline

Further down the road someone else had been watching the motorcade with more than usual interest. Jacqueline Dumas was twenty-six years old. She worked in a beauty salon and was on her way home. She was in a hurry to get ready for her evening date. In a few hours she knew she would be in the arms of her lover. She would go looking her best, but she hated him.

She came from a good family. They were very close to each other, her mother, her father and her brother, Jean-Claude. A few years before, Jean-Claude had been doing his national service. Near the end of 1959 his parents got a telegram. It was to say that Jean-Claude had died in Algeria. Jacqueline's happy world fell apart. The only thing that kept going through her mind was that her darling little brother had been shot dead. She began to hate.

Then François came. He turned up suddenly one Sunday

morning when her parents were away. She asked him what he wanted. He told her that he had been in charge of Jean-Claude's unit and that he had brought her a letter. She asked him in.

The letter was from Jean-Claude. He had written it just before he died. Jacqueline read the letter and cried a little. The letter was only about life in the Army, but François told her the rest – how he had taken a bullet through the lungs and died. François was very gentle with her. He asked her out to dinner and she went. She made him swear not to tell her parents about the way Jean-Claude had died. It was best that they should never know.

But she wanted to know more about the war in Algeria. President de Gaulle was supposed to be the man who would finish the war in Algeria. Her father loved the President. Hadn't de Gaulle promised to keep Algeria for the French? she asked François.

But François said that the President was not a hero, but a traitor.

They spent François's leave together. She met him every evening after work. On his next leave they met again and had a short time alone. Then in the spring of 1961 he came to Paris again. When they walked down the street together she thought he was the strongest, most handsome man in Paris. He was in uniform, she wore her prettiest dress. François was very excited about something. There was something in the wind. He promised that Algeria would be kept for the French. He went back to Algeria. He took part in the mutiny and was shot in a battle with a French Army unit. She was going to have his baby, but François never knew about it.

When Jacqueline heard that he was dead she tried to gas herself. She failed, but she lost the baby. Her parents took her away for a holiday and she seemed to be much better. In December she began to work for the OAS. Her aim was simple. The deaths of her brother and François must be paid for. No matter by what means or the cost to herself. This was her only reason for living.

In July 1963 a man came to see her. He would not give her his name. He asked if she would be willing to do a special job for the OAS. It could be dangerous and unpleasant. Of course, she said she would.

Three days later she was shown a man coming out of a block of flats. She was told who he was and what she had to do. By mid-July she had met him, seemingly by chance. She had watched him. She had followed him into a café and sat near him. She smiled at him and asked him for the salt. He had spoken to her, she had pretended to be shy. He was interested. Within two weeks they were lovers.

On the last day of that same month the Jackal was busy. He spent the morning at a Paris market where he bought a black beret, a pair of old shoes, some dirty old trousers and an old Army greatcoat. It was long on him, stretching to well below the knee – which was the important thing. He also bought some old Army medals.

After lunch in a café he went back to his hotel. He paid his bill and packed. He caught the train for Brussels at five-fifteen. He got there late at night.

12   A letter for big Viktor

The head of the Action Service sat at his desk and looked at the two papers in front of him. Both reports had come in that morning. One was from Rome. It told him that Rodin, Montclair and Casson were still in hiding in their top-floor hotel room. They were still under heavy guard. Extra police had been sent from Paris and Rome to keep watch on the hotel. Each day one of the guards left the hotel and walked to the main post office in Rome. The guard was a big man called

Viktor. He collected mail and took it back to the hotel. Rodin's name was not on the letters. He was using a code name.

The second report was about a police raid on a bar in a town called Metz. A man had half-killed two policemen. From his fingerprints they found him to be an OAS gunman wanted for murders in Algeria. His name was Sandor Kovacs. His partner in Algeria had been called Viktor. End of message.

The head of Action Service thought for a long time about the link between the two men. He sent for the file on Viktor. He read it slowly, then sent for a handwriting expert.

He told him, 'You and I are going to write a letter. We are going to do it with the help of someone who is not here at present – someone who will have to be made to help us.'

The letter to Viktor reached Rome on the morning of 1 August. Viktor had just got back to the hotel after his trip to the post office. He looked hard at his name on the envelope. No one was meant to know where he was. Viktor was not much of a reader. So he had not seen the item in the newspaper about three top OAS men living on the top floor of a Rome hotel. When he had handed in the day's post to Rodin he went to his own room to read his letter. He was surprised to find that it was from Sandor Kovacs. He had not seen him for a year, and in any case Sandor could hardly write.

The letter was not long. It told Viktor that his little girl, Sylvie, was very ill. She had cancer of the blood. Sandor said he hoped she would soon be better and that Viktor was not to worry.

But Viktor did worry. Sylvie's mother had been a call-girl in Marseilles. When she found that she was pregnant she told Viktor that the child was his. He believed her, perhaps because he wanted to. She also told him she did not want the child and knew an old woman who would get rid of it for her. Viktor hit her across the face, and told her that if she did he would kill her. Three months later he had to go back to Algeria.

In the meantime he became friendly with another man known as JoJo the Pole. JoJo had been wounded and was dis-

36

charged from the Army. He and his wife ran a snack stall. It was to JoJo that Viktor turned for help over the baby. The JoJos had no children of their own and said they would look after the child when it was born. This made Viktor very happy.

He saw his little girl only twice in his life. He first saw her when she was two and again when she was four. Viktor went with presents for the JoJos and toys for Sylvie. The small girl and her great big Uncle Viktor got on very well together.

And now she was sick. Viktor worried a lot through the rest of the morning. When he next went up to Rodin's office for his orders, he asked, 'What's cancer of the blood?'

Rodin said, 'I've never heard of it.'

From the other side of the room Casson said, 'Cancer of the blood. That's bad. There is no cure for it. Why?'

'Nothing,' muttered Viktor. 'Just something I read.'

Then he left. Rodin thought nothing of it. His mind was on something else. A letter had come by the afternoon mail to say that the OAS bank account now stood at over 250 000 dollars.

Viktor went down to the post office. He had to ask for help to get JoJo's phone number in France. He was not used to making calls to other countries.

At last he got through. JoJo said he was glad that Viktor had rung. He had been trying to find him for three months.

Sadly he said, it was true about the illness of little Sylvie. She had been getting weaker and thinner. She was in bed all the time now. 'How long do the doctors give her?' Viktor shouted down the line.

'It could be a week, maybe two or three,' JoJo said.

Viktor could not believe it. He stared at the phone in his hand. Without a word he put it back and walked out of the booth. He picked up the mail as usual and walked back to the hotel.

In his flat in France JoJo also put the phone down. He turned to the two men from the Action Service who were still standing there, each with his Colt .45 Police Special in his hand. One was pointing towards JoJo, the other on his wife.

'Bastards,' said JoJo, his voice full of hatred.

'Is he coming?' one of the men asked.

'He didn't say. He just hung up on me,' JoJo said.

'He had better come, for your sake, JoJo,' the man said.

'He will come,' JoJo said sadly. 'If he can, he will come. For the little girl's sake.'

'Good. Then your part is done.'

'Then get out of here,' shouted JoJo. 'Leave us alone.'

'You'll be coming with us,' the man said. 'We can't have you talking, or ringing Viktor back, now can we? Get packed. Bring the child in. Now move.'

'Where are you taking us?' asked JoJo.

'For a little holiday in the mountains. It will be good for you, JoJo,' the man said.

'For how long?' JoJo asked in a dull voice.

'For as long as it takes,' said the man.

13   A work of art

On the morning that Viktor got his letter, the Jackal left the hotel in Brussels. He took a taxi to the corner of the street where Mr Goossens, the gun-maker, lived.

Goossens let him in and locked the front door.

'Any problems?' the Jackal asked.

'The gun is ready,' Goossens said. 'It is a work of art. Let me show you.'

On the desk was a flat case about two feet long. Goossens opened the case. It had shaped spaces for the parts of the rifle that were in it. Along the top of the case was the barrel and breech, the whole no longer than eighteen inches. The Jackal lifted it out and looked at it. It was very light. He rammed the bolt home. Smoothly it locked into place.

The Jackal turned the rifle over. There was a narrow slit beneath the breech. Inside it was the stump of the trigger. Without a word Goossens handed him a small curved piece of steel. The Jackal put it into the slit and screwed it tight on to the stump. It was the new trigger.

Goossens took two steel rods from the case. 'This is the stock,' he said. The Jackal fitted the rods on. Goossens then handed him the butt-plate. It was about six inches long and padded with black leather. The Jackal clicked the butt into place. The rifle looked more normal now. He lifted the butt-plate to his shoulder. With his left hand he gripped the underside of the barrel. He put his right forefinger round the trigger. There was a soft click from inside the breech. Then they fitted on the silencer and telescopic sight.

The Jackal put the rifle down. He turned to Goossens and said, 'Very good. As you say, a work of art.'

Goossens smiled. He opened a drawer and took out some bullets. He put them on the desk.

A small part of the tip of each bullet had been cut away. A tiny hole had been drilled into the nose-cap. Into this hole a drop of mercury had been placed. Then the hole had been covered with a drop of lead. After the lead had gone hard, it was filed to a pointed shape, so that it looked just like an ordinary bullet.

But the Jackal knew about these bullets. They would go off like small grenades when they hit a human body. One hitting the head would shatter everything inside the skull.

'You are a craftsman,' the Jackal said. 'What about the tubes?'

'These have been harder to make than I thought,' Goossens said. 'I tried using very thin metal, but it bent when the slightest pressure was put upon it. So I had to use stainless steel. It looks the same but is stronger.'

Goossens placed on the desk a set of hollow steel tubes. He took the rifle apart and started to slide the parts into the tubes. Each part fitted perfectly. Then Goossens held up the tiny trigger and the six explosive bullets.

39

'I have had to find somewhere else for these,' he said.

He took the leather-padded butt of the rifle and showed the Jackal how the leather had been slit with a sharp knife. He pushed the trigger into the stuffing and closed the slit with a piece of black sticky tape. From the drawer he took a lump of black rubber. He fitted the six bullets into it and fixed it on to the last of the steel tubes. The bullets were now hidden from sight.

The Jackal took the tubes and shook them. But no sound came from them, for they were all lined with felt.

'Perfect,' said the Jackal. 'Just what I wanted.'

He took the steel tubes and packed them into an empty suitcase he had brought with him. Then he handed the fitted gun case back to Goossens. 'I shall not be needing that,' he said. He took the £700 from his pocket and put it on the desk.

'I think our deal is complete, Mr Goossens.'

Goossens picked up the money. 'Yes, unless there is anything else I can do for you.'

'Only one thing,' the Jackal said. 'Where in this country can I test the gun, without being seen?'

Goossens thought for a moment. Then he told him the name of a forest and how to get there. 'If you go there on a Monday it will be quiet. At the week-end people picnic there.'

'All right, thank you,' the Jackal said. 'And, Mr Goossens, you will please remember to be silent about all this.'

'I have not forgotten,' Goossens told him. 'It is the way I always work with people. I may say, I expect the same from you.'

The Jackal smiled. 'Then we understand each other. Good day, sir.'

The Jackal went back to his hotel and put the suitcase with the gun in it at the bottom of the wardrobe. He locked the wardrobe door and put the key in his pocket.

14　Blackmail

In the evening he paid a visit to the forger's studio.

'Finished?' the Jackal asked him when he went in.

'Yes, all finished,' the forger said, smiling. 'And very good work, even if I do say so myself.'

From his inside pocket he took a brown packet. He took three cards from it and spread them on the table. The Jackal took one of them and held it under the light. It was his driving licence. The first page was covered by a slip of paper which had been pasted on. The name printed on it was Alexander Duggan. So far as the Jackal could see it was a perfect forgery.

The second was a French identity card in the name of André Martin, aged fifty-three. It was a working man's card, dirty and crumpled. The photo on it showed his own face, but it looked much older and the hair was grey.

The third card interested him most. The photo on it was a little different from the other one. The date of issue was different by a few months. The shirt on the second photo was darker and there was a hint of stubble round the chin. Clever touching up had made the photos look like two pictures of the same man, taken at different times.

'Very nice,' the Jackal said. 'Just what I wanted. You have done well. Now, I still owe you fifty pounds.'

'That is true, sir. Thank you,' the forger said, and held his hand out for the money.

The Jackal took ten fivers from his pocket and handed them over, but before he let go of them he said, 'I think there is something more, yes?'

The forger pretended to looked puzzled.

'The front page of my driving licence – the old front page,' the Jackal reminded him. 'I said I wanted it back.'

The forger turned away. 'I thought we might be able to have a little chat about *that* piece of paper,' he said.

'Yes?' the Jackal said, giving nothing away.

'The fact is, my dear sir, that the old front page is not here. It is locked up in a deed-box in a bank. The box can only be opened by me.'

'What do you want?' the Jackal said coldly.

'Well now, my dear sir,' the forger said. 'I thought you might like to make me an offer for that piece of paper. Something rather more than the hundred and fifty pounds you talked about last time you were here.'

'I have met blackmailers before,' the Jackal said.

'Blackmail?' the forger said, pretending to be hurt by the word. 'Me? I only want one payment. After all, I have in my deed box not only that piece of paper, but the negs of the photos I took of you. I also have one other picture – one I took when you were not looking. It shows you with no make-up on. I am sure that those pictures, in the hands of the police, could make a lot of trouble for you. I am also sure that you are a man who is used to paying in order to avoid such trouble.'

'How much?' the Jackal asked shortly.

'One thousand pounds, sir.'

The Jackal nodded. 'It would be worth that much to me to get them back.'

The forger smiled. He was still smiling when the Jackal put his knee hard up between the forger's legs. The Jackal let him slip to the floor in agony. Then he slipped his right hand round the man's neck. He put his left hand against the back of the head. He gave one short, ugly twist to the neck, backwards, upwards and sideways. The forger's body went as limp as a rag doll. The tongue was half bitten through. The eyes were open and staring.

The Jackal opened the trunk in the corner of the room. He tipped out all the wigs and clothes and lifted the body into the trunk. Then he covered it with the clothes and wigs, shut the lid and padlocked it. He waited until darkness fell before he left. No one passed him as he slipped quietly down the street. Half a mile away he dropped the keys of the trunk down a large drain in the roadway.

15 Practice shots

The next day the Jackal went shopping. He bought a haversack, some sheets of thin foam rubber, a ball of string, a hunting knife and a string bag. Lastly, he bought two small paint brushes and two tins of paint, one of pink and one of brown.

On Monday morning the Jackal took the gun from his hotel wardrobe. He packed each part of it in layers of foam rubber and tied each one up with string. He put them all into the bottom of the haversack. On top went the tins of paint and brushes. The string bag went into one of the outer pockets. Into the other pocket he put a box of practice bullets. He then took the haversack down to the car he had hired in the name of Alexander Duggan. He locked the haversack inside the boot and drove off. By nine o'clock he was speeding out of Brussels. It was over ninety miles to the forest the gunsmith had told him about. Before noon he was on the winding road through the forest.

At last he found a narrow track running off into the forest. He turned the car a few yards up the track and stopped behind the cover of some bushes.

Slowly he got out, unlocked the boot, and took out the haversack. He took out the parts of the rifle and fitted them together. Then he took from the boot a large melon which he had bought the day before. He locked the car and set off into the forest on foot.

He found a long, narrow clearing in the trees. He took the paint and brushes and set to work on the melon. He painted the top and bottom of the melon brown; he painted the middle part pink. While the paint was still wet he drew in with his fingers a nose, eyes and a mouth. So as not to smear the paint, he stuck the hunting knife into the melon and carefully dropped it into the string bag.

Then he stuck the knife hard into a tree trunk. The knife

handle was about seven feet from the ground. He hung the string bag over the knife handle. The melon hung there like a great human head.

He threw the paint tins and brushes as far as he could into the bushes. Then he picked up the gun and paced out 130 metres from the tree. He slipped back the bolt and put a shell into the breech. Looking down the telescopic sight, he was pleased to see how big and clear his target looked. He took careful aim at the middle of the melon and fired.

The noise was hardly loud enough to be heard across a quiet street. He walked the length of the clearing to look at the melon. The bullet had gone through part of the handle of the bag.

He walked back again and fired a second shot. The result was almost the same. He tried two more shots but the gun was firing high and a little to the right. He changed the setting of the telescopic sight. The next shot went clean through the 'forehead'. From then on he shot each eye, the nose and the chin in turn.

He was pleased with the gun now. He took a tube of glue from his pocket and squeezed it over the heads of the screws that moved the sights. Half an hour later the glue had set hard. The sights were now set for his eyesight, with that gun, for a spot-on hit at 130 metres.

From his other pocket he took out an explosive bullet and slid it into the breech of the gun. He took careful aim, then fired. He walked down the clearing towards the tree. The string bag hung, limp and almost empty, against the trunk of the tree. The melon had been blown to bits, although it had stood up to fourteen practice bullets.

He took the string bag and threw it into the bushes. He pulled the knife out of the tree, picked up the gun and walked back to the car.

He was back in his hotel in Brussels soon after six o'clock. He cleaned every part of the gun and put it back into the suitcase. He paid his hotel bill and the bill for the hired car.

Then he packed and took a taxi to the main-line station. He left the suitcase in the left-luggage office.

He got the evening plane from Brussels to London. His rifle was at the left-luggage office in Brussels. Three well-forged cards were hidden in an inside pocket of his suit. It had all been worth the £1600 it had cost him.

16 Torture chamber

On that same Monday, Viktor was making another phone call at the post office in Rome. This time he was finding out the time of the planes from Rome to France. He had made up his mind. He would not be gone long, and he would tell Rodin everything when he got back. If he asked him first for leave, Viktor was sure that Rodin would say no. Rodin would not understand about little Sylvie.

He found out that the next possible flight was on Wednesday at eleven-fifteen in the morning. He sighed as he put down the phone. He was very upset at the thought of going absent without leave for the first time ever.

On Wednesday morning Viktor picked up the letters as usual and ran back to the hotel at full speed. He handed the post in to Rodin and was then free to go back to his room. He was not on duty again until that evening.

He stopped in his room just long enough to get his Colt .45 and put it into his shoulder holster (Rodin would never allow him to carry it in the street). A roll of notes that were his savings went into his pocket. He closed the door behind him. Once in the street he put on dark glasses.

At the café across the road a man with a newspaper looked over the top of it. He watched as Viktor looked up and down for a taxi. When one came, the man jumped up, got into a small Fiat and followed.

At the airport the man was still just behind Viktor. Viktor bought his ticket and soon after, his flight was called. The Secret Service man watched Viktor get on the plane, then went to a phone booth. He rang a number and said, 'He's gone, flight 451, landing at ten past twelve.' Twenty minutes later the message was passed on to Marseilles.

The plane touched down on time. As the passengers went through the customs hall they had to walk between two police-men sitting ten feet apart. A small bald man went up to one of them and whispered, 'Big fellow, black beret and dark glasses.'

When Viktor handed his passport over, the policemen hardly looked at him. The customs man stamped his passport and waved him on.

'Wonder what they want him for,' said one policeman to the other.

Viktor got on the airport bus which took him into the middle of Marseilles. Then it took him half an hour to find a taxi. Viktor told the driver to stop shortly before they got to JoJo's street. He walked the rest of the way and when he got to the block of flats, he took the steps at a run. He was eager to see Sylvie. Flat 23 had a bell with a little white card with JoJo's name on it. He pressed the bell.

The door in front of him swung open and a pick-axe handle swung out of the gap and down towards his head. It split the skin but bounced off the bone with a dull thud. The doors of flats 22 and 24 opened and men came out. It all happened in less than half a second. Viktor went mad. He knew how to fight, if nothing else.

Through the blood spurting over his eyes, he charged into flat 23. But the men closed in, grabbing for his jacket. Inside the room he drew the Colt from under his armpit, turned and fired into the doorway. The bullet ripped the knee-cap off one of the men. Then the gun dropped out of Viktor's hand as a cosh smashed down on his wrist. The other five men threw themselves at him. The fight lasted three minutes. Viktor must have taken more than twenty blows to the head from their coshes before he passed out. Part of his ear was cut off, his nose was broken and his face was covered in blood.

Twelve hours later, after a fast drive through the country-side, Viktor was lying in a prison cell. He was tied down to the bed, still out cold, but breathing.

The doctor turned to the man standing beside him.

'What did you hit him with?'

'It took six men to do that,' Rolland, the head of the Action Service, told the doctor.

'Well, they did a pretty good job. They nearly killed him,' the doctor said. 'If he wasn't built like a bull, they would have done.'

'I have to question him,' Rolland said.

The doctor looked at him in horror. 'If you start on him now, with your methods, he will either die or go mad. In any case, it will probably be a week before he even comes round.'

But the doctor was wrong. Three days later Viktor opened his eyes. He was taken to another cell and strapped to a heavy oak chair. In front of him, five men sat at a table. There was only one light in the place. It was very bright. The shade was turned so that it shone right at the chair. The rest of the cell seemed to be in darkness.

The prisoner had his legs tied to the chair with tight straps. The chair was bolted to the floor. Viktor's wrists were strapped to the chair arms. Another strap was round his waist. He was dripping with sweat.

In the table was a slit with a brass handle sticking up in it. The handle could be moved up and down the slit. Beside the slit was an on/off switch. The man at the end of the table had his hand near the switch.

Wires led from the table to a big socket in the wall. Little metal crabs with sharp teeth were stuck into Viktor's body. They were joined by wires to the on/off switch.

17 They always talk in the end

The cell was silent but for the sound of choking from the big man strapped to the chair. There was a smell of sweat, stale smoke, of metal and human vomit.

In the far corner, a single man sat at a wooden table, his face to the wall. In front of him was a tape recorder.

The man in the middle of the five at the big table spoke at last. His voice was gentle.

'Listen, Viktor. You are going to tell us. Not now, maybe, but in the end. You are a brave man. We know that. But even you cannot hold out much longer. So why not tell us? You know yourself, they always talk in the end. So why not now?'

Viktor lifted a tired face into the light. The eyes were closed. The mouth opened and tried to speak. Then the head sagged back on to the chest. As it did so, the shaggy hair shook from side to side in reply. The voice from behind the table spoke again.

'Viktor, listen to me. You have beaten the record already. But even you can't go on and on. But we can. If we have to, we can keep you alive for days, even weeks. There are drugs now, you know. So why not talk? We know about the pain. But the little crabs, they do not understand. They just go on and on. What are they doing in that hotel in Rome, Viktor?'

The great head was hung down on his chest and shook from side to side. At the far end of the big table the man moved the brass arm up the scale, from number 2 to number 4. Then he put the switch to 'ON'.

The little metal crabs came alive with a slight buzz. The great body in the chair rose. The legs and arms strained against the tight straps. It seemed as if the leather must cut clean through flesh and bone. The mouth was open as if in surprise. It was half a second before the horrible scream came out. When it did come it went on, and on, and on. . . .

Viktor broke at ten past four in the afternoon and the tape

recorder went on. As he started to talk, or rather to mutter, the calm voice of the man at the table broke in between the groans and cries.

'Why are they there, Viktor . . . Rodin, Montclair and Casson . . . what are they afraid of . . . who have they met up with . . . which hotel, Viktor . . . ?'

Viktor was at last silent after fifty minutes. Then it was clear that he would never speak again. It was all over.

The tape was rushed by fast car to the offices of the Action Service, just outside Paris. Three men sat round a tape recorder through the late afternoon and evening. They were trying to make sense of the muddle of words that had been Viktor's answers. Sometimes they would listen to a sentence ten times. One of them typed it out. It was nearly midnight when they finished and phoned the head of the Action Service.

Ten minutes later Rolland was on his way to the office. The top copy of Viktor's answers was brought in to him with some coffee. He read the twenty pages, trying to see what it was all about.

Rome came into it. The three leaders were in Rome. But he knew that already. But why?

Rolland went through it all again and again. The name 'Vienna' came in three times. They had a meeting in Vienna. Then they went into hiding in Rome. There were bits missing.

Rolland began to write down the bits that did not seem to fit in. The name 'Kleist'. A person? He rang the switchboard and asked them to look for a person or a place of that name in Vienna. The answer came in ten minutes. There were two pages of people called Kleist, a school of that name and a hotel.

Rolland noted the name of the hotel and then got on with the papers. There was something about a killer from abroad, and in another place the word 'blond'. It began to make sense. The word 'jackal' had been crossed out every time it cropped up – Rolland thought it was just Viktor's word for swearing at the men who had hunted him down. Now it took on a new meaning. It was the code name of a killer with blond hair. He must have come from abroad and met the OAS men at the Kleist Hotel in Vienna. Then the OAS leaders had gone into hiding in Rome.

Rolland could work out for himself the reason for all the bank raids of the last few weeks. The blond man, whoever he was, wanted money to do a job for the OAS. There was only one job in France that would get that sort of pay.

He locked the papers away, sent off an order to the Secret Service in Vienna and sat down to write a report.

The report ended, 'If the plot to kill the President of France is on, as I have described it, and if this killer has been hired, it is my duty to tell you that our country is in real danger.'

18   In the interests of France

The Minister of the Home Office sat at his desk later that morning. On the other side of the desk sat Jean Ducret, head of the President's personal guard. Ducret had stopped at least six plots to kill the President. At this moment he was reading through the report Rolland had sent to the Minister. As he finished reading, the Minister said, 'Well, what do you think, Ducret?'

'I think Rolland is right,' Ducret said. 'If what he says is true, this is a real plot. Our files on OAS men are useless if we are faced with an outside killer, working alone.'

The Minister ran his fingers through his grey hair. He was not a man easily upset, but he was upset this morning. He knew that the death of his President could cause riots and it was his job to keep law and order in France.

At last he said, 'Well, I must tell the President. I shall ask to see him this afternoon. Tell no one about this until I have seen him and know how the President wishes the affair to be handled.'

'The Minister is here, Mr President,' the ADC for the day said as he showed the Minister into the President's study.

There was nothing in the room that was not simple and in good taste. The tall man in the grey suit got up from his desk and held out his hand to greet the Minister.

'My respects, Mr President,' the Minister said and shook hands. He was shown to a chair in front of the desk. The President sat down. He leaned back, putting the tips of his fingers together on the desk in front of him. 'I am told that you wish to see me about a very important matter, my dear Minister.'

The Minister took a deep breath, and started to tell the story he had read in Rolland's report; about what Viktor had said; about the plot on the President's life; about the killer who might even now be making his plans.

When he had finished the President said, 'Well, my dear chap, what do you want me to do about it?'

The Minister took another deep breath and told the President what steps he thought should be taken. When he said, 'In the interest of France . . .' the President cut in.

'France!' he said in a deep voice. 'The interests of France are that the President of France should not be seen to be hiding from a murderer.' Then he added with even more feeling, 'A hired killer from outside.'

The Minister knew that he had lost. Two minutes later he left the President's palace. When he got back to his office he sent for the head of his staff, Alex, known to the Press as Mr Anti-OAS.

'He is impossible,' Alex said when he heard the Minister's news. 'We have to guard his life, but he won't let us. What do we do? Just wait for the Jackal to strike?'

'Listen, Alex,' the Minister said. 'First, we are not sure that Rolland's report is right. To start a nationwide hunt for a man known only by a code name is stupid at this stage. In that, I must agree with the President. He feels that if the secret were to come out, the Press would make a lot out of it. The President would be laughed at for hiding from a single man, a man from outside at that.'

'But,' Alex said, 'he must not appear in public again until the man is caught.'

'He will not agree to it,' the Minister told him. 'There will be no changes, not by even a minute. The whole thing has to be done in secret. We must find out who the killer is and he must be destroyed.'

'We must find out who the killer is, by secret means and destroy him. That, gentlemen, is the only course left open to us.' The Minister was speaking now to fourteen men who had been called for a special meeting. Among them was the head of the Secret Service; Rolland, head of the Action Service; Saint-Clair of the President's staff; and Bouvier, head of the Crime Squad.

The Minister spoke again to the fourteen men seated round the table. 'So that is where we stand, gentlemen. You have all read Rolland's report, and you have heard what the President has to say about it. Any action must be taken in secret. You will tell no one outside this room. Now I shall ask for your ideas on the matter. Rolland, have you had any luck with your searches in Vienna?'

'Yes,' Rolland told him. 'The clerk at the Kleist Hotel remembered the face of Rodin. He booked in on 15 June under another name. He had two visitors, who could have been Casson and Montclair. Another man joined them later for a short time. The clerk said he was tall and blond. He can remember nothing else. No name was given.'

'So now that Viktor is dead,' said one of the men, 'there are only four men in the world who know who the Jackal is – the man himself and the three OAS men in the hotel.'

'How about trying to get one of them back here?' someone said.

The Minister shook his head. 'My orders are that kidnap is out. What do you think, Bouvier?'

The head of the Crime Squad took his pipe out of his mouth and spoke slowly. 'It seems to me the first thing is to give this man a name. Even the OAS don't know who he is. The Action Service can't kill him, they don't know who to kill. The police can't arrest him, they don't know who to arrest. If we get a name, we get a face, with a face, a passport. Then an arrest. But to find the name, and to do it in secret is pure detective work.'

The Minister said quietly, 'And who is the best detective in France?'

Bouvier said, 'The best detective in France, gentlemen, is my own deputy, Claude Lebel.'

'Send for him,' ordered the Minister.

Part Two
The Manhunt

1 Enter Lebel

An hour later Lebel came out of the office looking tired. For fifty minutes he had listened to the Minister putting him in the picture. He had been given orders about what he had to do. They would all back him up. There would be no limits on money spent. The need for silence was explained to him several times.

While he listened his heart sank. They were asking the impossible of him. He had nothing to go on. There was no crime, not yet anyway. No clues. Just a code name, and the whole world to search in.

He had been promised that the police chiefs of other countries would be asked for help if need be. They might have killers like the Jackal on their files.

Claude Lebel was a very good detective. But he was not much to look at. He was small and rather shabby. In fact he looked like the cartoon pictures of henpecked husbands. No one in the force knew it, but that is just what he was. But he had a quick brain and was not easily frightened, even by the most ugly gang bosses in France.

As the men walked out of the office, Bouvier joined him and put a hand on his shoulder.

'So, my friend Claude, that's the way it is. Come, we'll talk in the car.'

In the car Bouvier said, 'You'll have to drop everything else. Operation Find-the-Jackal. Nothing else. Right? Is there anyone you want to help you?'

'Yes,' Lebel said, 'Caron, one of the young inspectors working with me.'

'OK, you have Caron. I'll fix that with the Minister. There's just one more thing. The whole group who were there tonight want a report from you, every evening at the Ministry. Ten o'clock sharp.'

'Oh, God,' Lebel said.

'You've just got to find this killer,' Bouvier said, 'before he gets to the President. From then on the Action Service boys will take care of things.'

The car drove through the gates of police HQ. Ten minutes later Claude Lebel was back in his office.

There was a knock on the door. It was Caron'. 'I just had a call from Bouvier's office. He told me to report to you.'

'Quite right,' Lebel said. 'Until further notice, I have been taken off all other duties and given a rather special job. You are to be my assistant.'

Lebel handed him the Rolland report. 'For a start, you had better read this.'

When he had finished reading it Caron looked up and said, 'God! They have dropped you in it. You know what they will do to you if you don't get this man in time?'

Lebel nodded sadly. 'I can't get out of it. I've been given the job. So from now on we just have to get on with it.'

'But where on earth do we start?' Caron asked him.

'We start by realizing that we have the most power ever given to two policemen in France,' Lebel said more cheerfully. 'So we use it. To start with get yourself set up behind that desk. Then get a camp bed sent in here and your washing and shaving tackle. We'll get a kettle and some coffee, sugar and milk. We are going to need a lot of coffee.'

'Tell the switchboard to leave ten outside lines for us, and one person on duty just for calls from this office. I also want direct links to the heads of police of Britain, America, Belgium, Holland, Italy, West Germany and South Africa. Get them at home or in the office. When you get through to each of them fix person-to-person calls starting at about seven in the morning. Allow twenty minutes for each call. That means I should get through the seven calls by about ten o'clock. They must be on the UHF wave-band. There must be no one listening in. Tell each of them that what I have to tell them is top secret. And say that's not only for the sake of France, but possibly for their own country, too.'

Caron looked up from the notes he was writing down. 'Yes, chief. I've got it. I had better get started.' He reached for the phone. As he did so the clock struck midnight.

2 Jacqueline at work

Saint-Clair got home just before midnight. He had just spent several hours typing out his report on the meeting at the Minister's office. He had not taken to Lebel. A silly little man, he thought. Not good enough to be given such an important task. He said so in his report which would be on the desk of the President's secretary in the morning.

He let himself in at the front door of his flat. He heard his new girlfriend call him from the bedroom. She had only moved in two weeks ago.

'Is that you, darling?' she called.

'Yes, dear. Of course, it's me. Have you been lonely?'

She came running from the bedroom and threw her arms round him. She was wearing only a thin nightdress.

He kissed her, and said, 'Get into bed and I'll join you.' He gave her a slap on the bottom.

Jacqueline hated him as much as on the day they had met. But she pretended to love him because he told her her about what went on at the President's palace, where he worked.

'Why were you so late?' she said when he came into the bedroom.

'Oh, nothing that you need worry your pretty head about,' he said.

'But I want to know,' she said. 'I've been lying here for hours worrying about you.' She turned away from him.

'Look, darling. I've been busy. There was something big on. I would have phoned you, but there were people in the office.'

'There couldn't have been anything so big that you couldn't have let me know,' she said.

'Well,' he said, 'it seems the OAS are still after the President.' He started to kiss her. 'They have hired a killer to get him. It is being taken care of. That's what kept me.' He then told her about the meeting.

Half an hour later Saint-Clair lay asleep. Jacqueline lay beside him staring up at the ceiling. What he had told her had shocked her. She waited until the bed-side clock showed two o'clock in the morning. Then she slid out of bed and went out of the bedroom. She closed the bedroom door very gently and quietly crossed the sitting room to the hall.

From the phone on the hall table she rang a Paris number. A sleepy voice answered. She spoke quickly for two minutes, then hung up. A minute later she was back in bed trying to get to sleep.

In a small flat in Paris, a middle-aged schoolteacher walked up and down. The flat was untidy, books and papers were all over the table, bed and chairs. But it was not the state of the flat that worried him. Since he had lost his job as a teacher, and his fine house with it, he had learned to live as he did now. He was worried about the phone call he had just taken. As dawn was breaking he made up his mind. He put on a light coat and left the flat. He stopped a passing taxi and went to the all-night post office near the station.

At the post office he placed a call to the Rome number he had been given, for use only in a crisis.

There were a number of clicks and then a tired voice said, 'Yes. . . .'

'Listen,' the schoolmaster said. He gave his code name, which was 'Valmy'. 'I don't have much time. Take a message : *The Jackal is blown. Viktor was taken, sang before dying.* That's it. Have you got it ?'

58

'Yes,' said the voice at the other end. 'I'll pass it on.'

Valmy put the phone back on the hook. Two minutes after he left, a car drew up outside the post office. Two men ran inside. They took a description from the switchboard man, but it could have fitted anybody.

In Rome, Rodin was woken by the guard who had been on duty all night on the floor below.

'A message,' the guard said. 'Someone phoned just now. Seemed in a hurry.' He handed Rodin a sheet from a pad. On it he had scribbled Valmy's message.

Rodin read the message and swore. He crumpled the bit of paper in his hand. Damn, damn Viktor.

For the first two days after Viktor went missing, Rodin thought that he had simply left his job. But he knew Viktor to be a loyal man. And here was proof that it had been a case of kidnap. Now it seemed he had talked, under torture of course. Rodin could imagine how he had died.

The important thing was to remember just what Viktor could have told them. The meeting in Vienna, the name of the hotel. Of course, all that. But what did he know about the Jackal? He could tell them of a tall blond man who had visited the three of them. That in itself meant nothing. There had been no name given. But Valmy's message gave the Jackal's code name. How could Viktor have told them that?

With a start of horror, Rodin remembered how he had stood at the door with the Englishman. Viktor had been a few feet down the corridor. What had he said? 'Good-bye, Mr Jackal.' Of course, blast it.

Thinking things over again, Rodin remembered that Viktor could not have known the killer's real name. Only himself, Casson and Montclair knew that. All the same, Valmy was right. The Jackal was blown. The police knew now about the meeting in the hotel, they had a code name, they would know the killer was tall and blond. The net around the President would be tighter than ever now. It was over. He would have to call the Jackal off and ask for the money back. The Jackal must be told.

59

He sent a guard to the main post office. The guard asked for a London number. When the phone at the other end began to ring the guard held on. He held on for half an hour. In the end he gave up, went back and told Rodin he could not get a reply.

Rodin told Casson, 'He's gone. He's on his way. We don't know where he is or what he is going to do next. He is on his own now. Nobody can stop the Jackal now. It's too late.'

3   Sorry, no reply

The Jackal had spent his first three days back in London shopping. He bought a set of three leather suitcases. Into one he put the clothes that would turn him into the Danish parson. He had sewn on to the parson's clothes the labels from the shirts bought in Denmark. Into the same case he put the clothes of the American student, Marty Schulberg. He slit the lining of the case and pushed two passports in – one in the name of the parson, the other in the name of Marty Schulberg. He also put in two sets of contact lenses wrapped in paper, and the hair dyes.

In the second case went the old overcoat and black beret and the army medals. In the lining of this case he hid the false papers of the old Frenchman, André Martin. The case was still half empty. The steel tubes with the rifle parts would go in later.

The last and smallest case was packed with the Alexander Duggan outfits – shoes, socks, shirts, ties and three smart suits. In the lining he hid £1000 in £10 notes.

He locked all the cases and put the keys on his key-ring. A light grey suit, cleaned and pressed, was left hanging in the wardrobe. Inside the breast pocket were his passport, driving licence and £100.

He also packed a small hand-grip with shaving gear, pyjamas and towel – also a bag of plaster of paris, several bandages, six rolls of sticking plaster, packets of cotton wool and a pair of strong shears. The grip would travel as hand luggage. He had noticed that airport customs men did not seem to bother with hand luggage.

He had reached the end of the planning stage. Now he had to wait to get two letters that would send him on his way. One was to tell him the Paris phone number which he could use. The other letter would tell him that 250 000 dollars had been paid into his bank account.

While he was waiting, he kept walking round the flat with a limp. The first letter came on 9 August. It gave him the Paris phone number and told him to say, 'Jackal here' when he phoned. The reply would be 'Valmy here'.

The other letter came on 11 August. He grinned as he read that the money was in his bank. As long as he stayed alive, he was a rich man for the rest of his life.

He spent the rest of that morning booking flights on the phone.

The next morning he got up early. He checked his three suitcases. Only the hand-grip had to be filled up with his washing and shaving gear. He drank two cups of coffee, washed and shaved. He put on a silk polo-neck shirt, the light grey suit, dark socks and black shoes. He checked that the passport and driving licence in the name of Duggan were in the breast pocket of his suit. Then he put on a pair of dark glasses.

At nine-fifteen he took his cases, locked the door of the flat behind him and went downstairs. He caught a taxi on the corner of the street. 'London Airport, Number Two Building,' he told the driver.

As the taxi moved away the phone in his flat began to ring, and ring, and ring. . . .

4 Interpol

Lebel got back to his office at six in the morning. He had spent the night searching through files in Criminal Records. Caron was still at his desk, his sleeves rolled up, looking very tired. Lebel sank into a chair.

'Nothing,' he told Caron. 'I've been through the lot over the past ten years. The only hired killer from abroad who ever tried to do a job here is dead now. Central Records are doing a double check, but I doubt that we have this man on our files. The OAS leaders would make sure of that before they hired him. But a killer of this sort must have got his training somewhere. He must be one of the world's experts. That means someone must have a file on him, somewhere. What about those phone calls. Have you fixed them?'

'Yes, all seven are fixed,' Caron said. 'You start with Washington at ten past seven and end with Rome at nine-thirty.'

'You got the top man in every case, did you?' Lebel asked.

'Yes, with Scotland Yard it's Tony Mallinson. . . .'

Lebel cut him short. 'We had better go. Come on.'

It was ten to seven when they drew up outside Interpol HQ. For the next three hours, Lebel and Caron sat hunched over the phone talking to the world's top crime chiefs. Detective spoke to detective across the world. To each one, Lebel's message was much the same. 'It's just a tip-off at the moment. Top secret. We are looking for one of the world's most expert killers. We know very little about him apart from that. He is tall and blond. We want to know if you have anyone like that on your files.'

Lebel knew that they would all guess that the target was the President of France. The answers were much the same in each case. 'Yes, of course. We'll do our best. We'll go through all our files for you. I'll try and get back to you before the day is over. Good luck.'

When he had put the phone down for the last time, Lebel

wondered how long it would be before the Prime Ministers of the seven countries would get to hear about it. Even a policeman had to report something as big as that to the Minister.

Caron watched him quietly. 'Come on,' he said, 'Let's get some breakfast.'

'Yes, and some sleep,' agreed Lebel. 'There's not much more we can do just now.'

At Scotland Yard, Mallinson put down the phone with a frown. There was no doubt in his mind what Lebel had been talking about. He felt sorry for Lebel and the job he had been given. Plainly he was trying to guard President de Gaulle, but not allowed to mount a public manhunt.

He pressed one of the buttons on the intercom, 'I want you to get on to Central Records. Tell the chief that I want him to check every record of hire-killers known to be living in Britain. And tell him I can't explain at the moment why I am asking.'

The reply came just before noon. 'It seems there's no one on Criminal Records who fits, sir. The super suggests you get on to Special Branch.'

Mallinson typed out a report to Special Branch. It ended, 'Criminal Records reports that no one to fit the man Lebel is looking for could be found in their files. So the matter is being passed to Special Branch.'

5 A bad leg

The Jackal landed in Brussels just after twelve. He left his luggage in a locker at the airport. He kept the hand-grip with him. He took a taxi to the main station and went to the left-luggage office.

The suitcase with the gun in it was still on the shelf. He handed in his ticket and was given the case back.

Not far from the station he found a small, shabby hotel. He took a single room for the night and took his case and grip up to his room himself. He locked the door and filled the basin with cold water. Then he put the plaster and bandages from his hand-grip on to the bed. He set to work putting his leg in plaster as if it had been broken.

It took over two hours for the plaster to dry when he had finished. During this time, with his heavy leg and foot resting on a stool, he smoked several filter-tip cigarettes. Every so often he would test the plaster with his thumb to see if it was hard enough.

The suitcase that had held the gun lay empty. When at last he was ready, he slid the empty suitcase under the bed. He checked the room for any tell-tale signs, made sure that the wash-basin was clean, and threw the stubs from the ash-tray out of the window.

He found that the heavy plaster on his leg made him limp. He went downstairs. He was very glad to see that the desk clerk was in the back room behind the desk. He checked the front door to make sure no one was coming in. Then he clutched his hand-grip to his chest and crawled past on all fours.

He limped down the steps and along the street to the corner. A taxi spotted him inside half a minute. He was on his way back to the airport.

He went to the counter, passport in hand. He said to the girl, 'You have a ticket for Milan – reserved for me two days ago – name of Duggan.'

She checked the bookings for the afternoon flight to Milan. It was due to leave in a couple of hours.

The Jackal paid in cash and was told he would be called in about an hour. A porter helped him to get his suitcases from the locker, making a fuss over him because of his plastered foot. The cases were passed through customs. He spent the rest of the waiting time having a good lunch in the airport dining room.

All the flight staff were very kind to him because of the leg. He was helped on to the coach out to the plane, and again as he went on board.

At four-fifteen the plane took off, heading south for Milan.

The Jackal's plane touched down at the airport in Milan soon after six. The hostess helped him down the steps. Then he had to go through customs. It was here that his careful work in hiding the parts of the gun paid off. As the suitcases from the plane came along the moving belt the risks began to mount.

The Jackal got a porter to put the three cases into a line, side by side. The Jackal put his hand-grip down beside these.

'This is all your baggage, sir?' one of the customs men asked.

'Yes, these three cases and this little bag,' said the Jackal.

'Have you anything to declare?'

'No, nothing,' the Jackal told him.

The customs man said, 'Please open this one.'

The Jackal took out his key ring and opened the suitcase. It was the one that held the clothes of the Danish parson and the American student. The Customs man went through the clothes quickly. He did not look closely at the sewn-up slit in the lining of the case. The parts of a complete sniper's rifle were only three feet away from him across the desk. But he did not know it. He told the Jackal to shut the case, then he chalked all the luggage with a cross.

The porter found a taxi and was well tipped for it. Soon the Jackal was speeding into Milan. He asked to be taken to the Central Station.

Here another porter was called. The Jackal hobbled after him to the left-luggage office. In the taxi he had slipped the steel shears from the hand-grip into his trouser pocket. At the left-luggage office he left the hand-grip and two suitcases. He kept with him the case that held the long army overcoat. There was plenty of spare room in it besides.

He limped into the men's toilet and locked himself inside

one of the cubicles. With his foot up on the toilet seat, he clipped at the plaster for ten minutes until it began to drop away. When the foot was clear he put back on the sock and shoe which had been taped to his leg, inside the plaster. The rest of the plaster he flushed down the toilet.

He put the suitcase on top of the toilet seat. He wiped the last bits of plaster from the set of steel tubes that held the rifle parts. Then he placed them in the case among the folds of the big overcoat. Then he locked the case and looked outside the door. There were two people standing at the wash-basins. He came out and made quickly for the door. He was up the steps into the main hall of the station before they had time to see him.

He could not go back to the left-luggage office a fit man after just having limped there as a cripple. So he called a porter, told him that he was in a great hurry, and asked the porter to go and get his baggage while he changed some money. He put the baggage ticket into the porter's hand along with a thousand-lire note.

The porter nodded happily and went off towards the left-luggage office. The Jackal changed £20 into Italian lire and was just finished when the porter came back with the cases. Two minutes later he was on his way to a grand hotel.

At the desk in the hotel lobby he told the clerk, 'You have a room for me. My name is Duggan. It was booked by phone from London two days ago.'

He was shown to his room and soon after he was having a shave and shower. Two of the suitcases were locked in the wardrobe of his hotel room. The third, with his own clothes in, lay on the bed. He was looking forward to a drink, a good dinner, and an early night. He had a lot to do tomorrow.

By nine the next morning the Jackal was in a hardware shop. He bought a pair of wire cutters, several yards of thin steel wire and a soldering outfit. Then he found a row of lock-up garages in a working-class part of the city. He hired one of them.

After lunch he went to a car-hire firm. He told them that he was touring Italy for the next two weeks. He hired a 1962 Alfa-Romeo two-seater. He drove the Alfa back to the hotel and went up to his room. He waited until all was quiet. Then he took the suitcase with the rifle parts in it down to the car and locked it in the boot.

Shortly after tea-time he was back at the garage he had hired. He locked the door behind him and got to work. It took him two hours to weld the steel tubes holding the rifle to the underside of the Alfa's body-work. When he had finished the tubes could not be seen. He put the soldering iron under a pile of old rags in the corner of the garage. The metal clippers went into the glove box of the car. He locked the door after him and drove back to the hotel.

He was ready now to drive through Italy and over the border into France. He had the car, and the gun was well hidden underneath it.

6   Progress report

Superintendent Bryn Thomas of Special Branch closed the last of the folders with a sigh. 'Right, that's it, then,' he said to the detective who had been helping him check the files. 'Pack up the files. I'll say that we have made a careful search and that no such man is known to us. That's all we can do.'

The detective picked up the files and went out. Bryn Thomas started to write his report. He was very proud of Scotland Yard's good record, and even more proud of the Special Branch. They had never had any trouble of this kind. They had never lost a visiting VIP – never even had any scandal, let alone a killing. Thomas had two years to go before he retired – two years until he could go back and settle in Wales.

Perhaps this man the French were looking for *was* British. Better be safe, check everything.

He picked up the phone and asked for a man he knew through his golf club. Thomas knew that this man, Barrie Lloyd, was working for the Secret Service.

The two men met that evening for a drink in a pub down by the River Thames.

'Got a bit of a problem, boyo,' Thomas told Lloyd. 'Hoped you might be able to help.' Thomas told him what they were looking for. 'I just thought he might be the kind of killer who behaves himself in this country, and keeps off our records. But if he had done any jobs abroad the Secret Service might have heard about it.'

Lloyd stared out over the dusky river. 'There was a killing two years ago. In the West Indies. It was one hell of a shot, from one hundred and thirty metres at a speeding car. The story goes that the marksman was an Englishman. It was only talk.'

Thomas said, 'But a report must have been filed at the time. Was there a name?'

Lloyd said, 'I can look back through the files for you. You get on home. I'll ring you if anything comes up.'

'I'd be glad if you would,' Thomas said. They finished their drinks and left.

It was just after midnight when Barrie Lloyd rang Thomas back. 'I found the report we were talking about,' he said. 'Just a report, marked, "No Action to be Taken".'

'Any name given?' Thomas asked.

'Yes, an Englishman in the West Indies went missing around that time. He might have had nothing to do with it. But there was talk about him at the time. Name of Charles Calthrop.'

Thomas said, 'Thanks, Barrie. I'll follow it up in the morning.'

While Thomas and Lloyd had been drinking together, Lebel was at the first progress meeting in Paris. The same fourteen men at the Ministry. The Minister spoke first.

He told them that checks were being made on every border post in France. The guards had been told to look out for tall blond men in particular. All luggage was to be searched and passports checked for forgery.

The others gave their reports. Criminal records had found no hired killers outside the ranks of the OAS.

The chief of police then made his report. At seven-thirty that morning they had tracked a call from a post office near a Paris railway station. They had traced it to the hotel in Rome where the three OAS heads were staying. The message had been: 'Valmy calling. The Jackal is blown. Viktor was taken. Sang before dying.'

There was silence in the room for several seconds.

'How did they find out?' Lebel asked quietly from his end of the table.

All eyes turned on him. Then Rolland suddenly said, 'Blast! To get Viktor to come from Rome, we used his old friend, JoJo, as bait. We kept the JoJo family prisoner until we got Viktor. All we wanted from Viktor was to find out what the OAS chiefs were up to. We did not suspect this Jackal plot at the time. So we let the JoJos free after Viktor sang. It must have been JoJo who told the agent, Valmy. Sorry.'

'Did the police pick Valmy up at the post office?' Lebel asked.

'No, we missed him by a couple of minutes,' the police chief said.

'In a way,' the Minister said, 'it might be just as well they know their killer is blown. Surely they must call the plot off now.'

'He isn't really blown,' Lebel said. 'We still don't know the man's name. The warning might simply make him take more care.'

The Minister nodded. 'I think we had better have Lebel's report now,' he said. 'After all, he is in charge. We are here to help him where we can.'

Lebel told them of the Interpol calls to seven countries. 'The replies came in during the day,' he said. 'Here they are:

69

Holland, nothing. Italy, several known hire-killers, but all working for the Mafia. The Mafia would not agree to kill a President of another country. Britain, nothing – but it has now been passed on to Special Branch for further checks. Nothing very helpful from any of the other countries.'

The Minister said, 'Then there's nothing more to report. I can only ask you all to go on helping, as you have done over the last day. Until tomorrow at the same time, gentlemen.' The Minister got up and the meeting broke up. Outside the clocks struck midnight.

7   Find Charles Calthrop

Bryn Thomas had spent the morning and most of the afternoon trying to track down a man. All he knew about the man was a name, Charles Calthrop. He had started with the passport office. There he had found passport forms for six different Charles Calthrops. But they all had middle names, and all were different. He had also got a copy of the passport photos of all of them.

One of the passports was too new to count. One man was far too old. But the other four were possibles. Two of the addresses were in London, the other two in other towns. During the morning the police got on to the two who lived outside London. One had been away only once, to Spain for a holiday. Neither of them had ever been to the West Indies.

One of the Charles Calthrops who lived in London turned out to be a grocer. He didn't even know where the West Indies were. The fourth and last Calthrop was proving more difficult to find. The address turned out to be a block of flats in Highgate. But he had left there and no one knew his new address. But at least Thomas knew his middle name – he was Charles Harold Calthrop.

Through the GPO Thomas found out this Charles Calthrop's new address. At this point a visit was made to the flat. It was locked and there was no answer when the bell was rung. Nobody else in the block seemed to know where Mr Calthrop was. Thomas tried a new tack. He asked the income tax office to check their records to see who Calthrop had worked for over the past three years.

It was at this moment that the phone rang. Thomas picked it up and listened. Then he said in surprise, 'Me? What, in person? Yes, of course. I'll come right away.' He put the phone down. So it had reached the Prime Minister's ears already.

Thomas walked down to No. 10 Downing Street. He was shown in by a policeman who took him down a corridor. A secretary opened the door for him and showed him into the Prime Minister's office.

The Prime Minister said, 'Please sit down. I have heard that you have been asked to help the French police.'

'Yes, Prime Minister.'

'And this is because the French police are afraid that a man may be on the loose – a hired killer – to do a murder in France. It does not take much to guess that they fear the target is the President of France.'

Thomas said, 'Yes, sir. There have been six tries already.'

'How far have you got?' the Prime Minister asked him.

Thomas told him about the searches in Criminal Records and from there how it had been passed to Special Branch. He told him the lead he had got from Lloyd, and the search for a man called Charles Calthrop.

When he had finished the Prime Minister said, 'Thomas, I wish you to know that the President of France is my friend. If there is the slightest danger to his person from an Englishman, then that Englishman must be stopped. From now on you will have my full help. No limits will be placed on what your team is allowed to do. Money and manpower are yours for the asking. You will, on my orders, help the French police in every way you can. Only when you are quite sure that this killer is not British, nor working from this country, will you call off the hunt. Do I make myself clear?'

It could not have been clearer.

Back in Thomas's office things changed quickly. He gathered round him a task force of six of the best Special Branch detectives. He put them all in the picture and told them it all had to be kept quiet.

It was just after six in the evening when the telephone rang. It was the income tax office. They had found the tax returns of Charles Harold Calthrop. One of the detectives was sent to bring the whole file. Another detective went off to Calthrop's flat. His job was to question everyone who lived nearby who might know where Calthrop was. Every detective was given a copy of the photo from Calthrop's passport form, taken four years ago.

The tax returns showed that Calthrop had been out of work for a year. Before that he had been overseas for a year. But for most of the year before that he had been working for a firm that made small firearms. Thomas phoned the boss of the firm and fixed a meeting with him. His name was Patrick Monson.

Patrick Monson hardly looked like a dealer in deadly weapons. But then, Thomas thought to himself, they never do. From Monson, Thomas found out that Calthrop had worked for the firm for just under a year. More important, in December 1960 the firm had sent him to the West Indies. His job was to try and sell a stock of ex-Army submachine-guns to the police chief of one of the islands.

'Why did Calthrop leave the West Indies in such a hurry?' Thomas asked.

Monson seemed surprised at the question. 'Well, because the ruler of the island had been killed, of course. The rebels had taken over and Calthrop had to get out. After all, he was trying to sell guns to the other side.'

That made sense, Thomas thought. Then he asked Monson, 'Why did Calthrop leave the firm?'

'He was sacked,' Monson said. 'Let us just say, we were not quite sure that Calthrop was loyal to the firm.'

In the car on the way back into town Thomas thought over what Monson had told him. It did not seem very likely that Calthrop's name was linked with the murder. On the other hand he could have been double-crossing the firm. Could he have been in the pay of the rebels, while pretending to sell arms to the other side? There was no proof either way. But Calthrop could have learned to handle guns expertly while he was working for the firm.

When he got back to the office one of the detectives was waiting for him. He had found a woman living in the flat next to Calthrop's. She had told him that Mr Calthrop had left for a holiday in Scotland a few days ago. She had seen what looked like a set of fishing rods in the back of his car.

Fishing rods? Thomas suddenly went cold when he heard that, though the office was quite warm.

8 A passport to the West Indies

In Paris the third meeting at the Ministry began just after ten o'clock. Lebel's report was bad. All the seven countries had reported back. Their further searches had shown nothing of any use. For one reason or another, none of the men on their files could be the Jackal. 'There's nothing,' Lebel ended. 'We are back to where we started.'

At that moment there was a knock on the door. The Minister had given orders that no one was to disturb them. 'Come in,' he said crossly.

One of the porters stood in the doorway, 'I'm sorry, Minister. A phone call for Mr Lebel. It's from London. They say it is urgent.'

Lebel went out and was back in a few moments. He had a piece of paper in his hand. 'I think, gentlemen,' he said, 'we have the name of the man we are looking for. Charles Calthrop.'

The meeting ended half an hour later, in a much more cheerful mood. Each man knew that, at least, there was something they could do now. They had agreed to search the whole of France for a man called Calthrop. They would have to do it without the public getting wind of what was on. They would find him, and, if need be, get rid of him.

The full files on Calthrop would not be ready until morning. But in the meantime checks could be made at hotels. His name and photo could be given to the border guards and to the police at airfields and ports. They would be given orders to arrest him. If he had not yet reached France, no matter. When he did they would have him.

Saint-Clair told Jacqueline that night as they lay in bed, 'This terrible man called Calthrop – we have him in the bag already.'

When Saint-Clair was asleep, Jacqueline made herself stay awake. Then she got up and went to the hall phone.

Back in London Thomas had called in the six detectives from their various jobs. He had just phoned Paris with the news about Calthrop.

Now he told his six assistants what they had to do next. One was to check on Calthrop's childhood; where his parents now lived; where he had been to school; his shooting record, if any. Another detective was to check on Calthrop's record in the Army and his record at the firm where he had worked until he was sacked.

Two more were put on the trail of what he had been up to since he left the firm; where he had been; who he had seen; what his income was; where the money had come from. There was no police record. So Thomas needed to get hold of any photos of the man that could be found. The last two detectives had to find out where Calthrop was at the present time. They were to go over to his flat for fingerprints; find out where he bought his car; check driving licence records; trace the car and find out the make, colour and number. They were also going to find his local garage; check if he was planning a long journey by car; check the cross-Channel ferry bookings and airline bookings.

All six men took down a lot of notes. Then they left the office. Outside one of them said, 'The odd thing is, that the boss won't tell us what he's supposed to have done – or is going to do. To get this sort of action, you'd think he was planning to shoot the King of Siam.'

It took only a short time to get a search warrant. In the small hours of the morning two detectives went through Calthrop's flat with a fine tooth comb.

They were both experts at the job. They started with drawers. They tipped the contents of each one into a sheet and sorted through everything. Then they started work on the desk, looking for secret panels. They ripped open the chairs and sofa.

By six in the morning the flat was as clean as a whistle. One of the detectives came out with a suitcase full of Calthrop's papers and personal belongings. He jumped into the waiting squad car and drove back to the office to report to Thomas. The other detective stayed at the flats. He was going to question the other people living in the flats.

Thomas spent several minutes going through the things from the case. The detective who had brought the case back was helping him. He picked a small blue book up and started to look through the pages. Suddenly he said, 'Super, have a look at this.' He pointed at one of the pages in the passport. 'See . . . West Indies, 1960. He was there all right. This is our man.'

Thomas took the passport from him. 'Oh yes, this is our man. But we are holding his passport in our hands.'

'So he isn't travelling with his own passport,' the detective said.

'As you say,' Thomas said. 'If he is not travelling on this passport, then what is he travelling on? False papers? Get me Paris on the phone.'

Thomas thought for a moment. 'Then the next thing to do is to get two or three of you down to the passport office. Get a complete list of every passport made out in the last month or so. Then if there's nothing, go back through another month. It's going to be a hard grind.' He told the detective the most common way of getting hold of a false passport. (It was, in fact, the method the Jackal had used.)

'Don't just check the birth records, check the deaths as well. If you can find a passport form filled in by a man who isn't alive any more – we are on to him. Off you go.'

It was two hours later that one of the detectives phoned back. 'There are eight thousand passports that have been made out in the last three months. It's the summer holidays, you know.'

Thomas hung up. 'Blast summer,' he said.

9   The Jackal enters France

By this time the Jackal was out on the road from Milan. The hood of the Alfa was down. He pushed the car to well over eighty miles an hour. The day's traffic was already thick when he got to the French border, and the heat was rising.

He had to wait for nearly half an hour at the border. Then he was called up to the parking ramp for customs check. The policeman who took his passport looked at it carefully. 'One moment, sir,' he said, and went into the customs shed. He came out a few minutes later with a man in plain-clothes who was holding the passport in his hand.

'Good morning, sir. This is your passport?' the man asked.

'Yes,' the Jackal nodded.

'What is the reason for your visit to France?'

'I am on holiday.'

'I see. The car is yours?'

'No. It is hired. I had business in Italy. Then I had a week with nothing to do. So I hired a car to do a little sight-seeing in France.'

'I see. Have you the papers for the car?'

The Jackal showed his driving licence and the hire-form. The plain-clothes man looked at them both.

'Have you any luggage, sir?'

'Yes. Three cases in the boot, and a hand-grip.'

'Please bring them all into the customs hall.' He walked ahead. The policeman helped the Jackal unload the luggage. Together they carried it to the customs.

Before he left Milan the Jackal had taken the old Army overcoat and the dirty trousers out of one of the cases. He had rolled them up tightly and stuffed them right at the back of the boot. The medals were in his pocket. The clothes from the other two cases had then been shared out among the three cases.

The customs men looked through each case. While they were doing so the Jackal filled in the form he was given. It was the usual form for holiday-makers entering France. Nothing unusual was found in the cases.

Out of the corner of his eye, the Jackal could see through the window. Another man was searching the boot and bonnet of the Alfa. Luckily, he did not look underneath. He unrolled the overcoat and trousers in the boot. He looked at them with disgust. He thought the coat must be for covering the bonnet on winter nights, and that the old trousers were in case running repairs had to be done to the car. He put them all back into the boot.

The customs men inside the shed closed the cases and handed the Jackal his passport.

'Thank you, sir. Have a good holiday.'

By about eleven that morning the Jackal stopped in the middle of a big town. He parked outside a hotel and went into the lobby. He went up to the desk and said to the clerk, 'Can you get me a Paris number on the phone, please?'

'Yes, what number did you want?' she said.

He told her the number. She went to the switchboard and made a sign to the Jackal to take the call in a booth close by.

He went in and closed the sound-proof doors.

'Hello, Jackal here,' he said.

'Hello, Valmy here,' came the reply. 'Thank God you have rung. We've been trying to get hold of you for days. Now listen. . . .'

When the call was finished, the Jackal went back to the desk and paid the charge. Then he asked for a pot of coffee, and when it came he took it out into the garden. He was deep in thought.

The bit about Viktor he could understand. He remembered the giant of a guard at the hotel in Vienna. What he could not understand was how Viktor had known his code name. And how did Viktor know what the meeting with the three OAS heads was about? Perhaps Viktor had guessed that he had been sent for a killing. Or perhaps the French police had put two and two together from what they got out of Viktor.

The Jackal tried to sort it all out. Valmy had said he ought to quit and go back to England. But he knew something they did not know; and something that the French police could not know either. It was that he was travelling under a false name. He had a passport in that name, and he also had three different sets of false papers and disguises to match. Also the French police were hunting for a man called Charles Calthrop. Then let them hunt, and good luck to them. He was Alexander Duggan, and he could prove it .

With Viktor dead, no one, not even Rodin, knew where he was or who he was. He was on his own at last. And that was the way he had always wanted it.

But there was more danger now. There was no doubt of that. The question was still there : to go back, or to go on? To go back would be to argue with Rodin and his bunch of thugs over the money at present in his Swiss bank. If he refused to hand it back, they would track him down and kill him. To go on would mean more and more danger until the job was done.

The bill came and he frowned when he saw it. God, the prices these people asked. To live this kind of life a man needed to be rich. Over the past three years he had tasted rich living.

He was used to good clothes, a smart flat, a sports car, smart women. To go back meant giving it all up.

He paid the bill and left a fat tip. Then he got into the Alfa and drove off into the heart of France.

10   The Baroness

The Jackal was in no great hurry. The day he had set for the kill was not yet here. He had reached France with time to spare. Even in the heat, the air in the hills was sweet and cool. As dusk was falling he reached the little town of Gap. He could have gone on, but there was no hurry. He found, at last, an old hunting-lodge just outside the town. There were rooms still free. He took one with a bathroom. After his bath he put on his dove-grey suit with a silk shirt.

Dinner was served in a lovely old room looking out over the woods. Half-way through the meal, a woman asked the head waiter to close the windows as she found the air chilly. She was a handsome woman in her late thirties. She had a good figure and was wearing a low-cut dress without sleeves. Her arms were soft and white. The Jackal turned to look at her. She answered with a cool smile.

The dinner was splendid. As he finished, he heard the low voice of the woman telling the waiter, 'I will take coffee in the lounge.' The waiter bowed and said, 'Of course, Baroness.' A few minutes later the Jackal also asked for his coffee to be served in the lounge.

An hour later, the Baroness stopped at the door of her room and turned to the young Englishman. He had insisted on seeing her to her room. It had been a pleasant evening. She was still not quite sure whether to insist that it end there.

She was a married woman and was not in the habit of asking

total strangers into her room. On the other hand she was nearly forty, and her marriage was over, in all but name. The Baron was too busy chasing girls in Paris. She felt suddenly very lonely. She had been thinking about her future, when the Englishman had come over and asked if he might take his coffee with her. She was pleased and was too surprised to say no.

After ten minutes with him she was glad she had agreed. He was good-looking and had made her laugh. Although he was English, he spoke very good French.

'It has been a very pleasant evening,' she said to him. Her hand was on the door handle. She wondered if he would try to kiss her. In a way she hoped he would. She felt his arm slip round her back and his lips came down on to hers. She found herself liking his kisses. She knew that she wanted him. He opened the door, and she stepped backwards into the room. 'Come in, stranger,' she said.

The finger of light from the moon lit up the dress and stockings that had been flung on the floor. The Baroness lay on her back, running her hand through the blond hair of the man beside her. She smiled as she thought back over the night. She looked at the clock by her bed. It said a quarter past five.

'Hey,' she said. 'I have to get up in two hours to drive home. And you have to go back to your room, my little Englishman.'

He got off the bed and started to get dressed. Then he sat on the edge of the bed and put his arms round her neck.

'It was good?' he asked.

She said, 'It was very good.' She laughed. 'I don't even know your name.'

Thinking quickly, he told her, 'Alex.'

'And mine is Colette,' she said.

He bent down and kissed her. 'In that case, good night, Colette.'

A second later he was gone and the door closed behind him.

At seven in the morning a policeman went into the hotel lobby.

'Hello,' the owner of the hotel said. 'You're bright and early.'

'As usual,' the policeman said. 'It's a long ride out here on a bike. I always leave you till the last.'

'I know,' the owner said. 'That's because we do the best coffee round here. Marie, bring the officer a cup of coffee.'

The policeman grinned.

'Here are the cards,' the owner said. He handed over the little white cards filled in by people who had booked into the hotel. 'Only three new ones last night.'

The policeman put the cards in the pouch on his belt. 'Hardly worth turning up for,' he said. 'Still, orders are orders.'

It was after eight when he got back to the police station at Gap and handed the cards in. From there they would be sent on to police HQ in Paris.

As the policeman was handing in the hotel cards, the Baroness was paying her bill back at the hotel. Then she got into her car and drove off. The Jackal slept on until nine o'clock.

11 On to Duggan

The call from the detective working at the passport office came at a quarter past ten. Thomas answered the phone. 'You sound tired,' he said to the man on the other end.

'Yes, we are,' the detective said. 'But we've found something. Alexander James Duggan.'

'What about him?' Thomas asked.

'Well, he was born on 3 April 1929. Filled in a passport form in the normal way on 14 July this year. The passport was sent to him by post three days later. It's probably not his own home address.'

'Why?' asked Thomas.

'Because,' the detective said, 'Alexander James Duggan was

81

killed in a car crash at the age of two, in November 1931.'

Thomas was quiet for a moment. Then he said, 'How many more passports still to check?'

'About three hundred,' the voice at the other end said.

'Leave them for the rest of the team to go on checking, just in case there is another false one,' Thomas told him. 'I want you to check out that address – the one the Duggan passport was posted to. Call me back the minute you find it. If there is anyone living there, talk to them. Bring me back all you can find about this so-called Duggan. And bring me a copy of his passport photo. I want to have a look at this lad Calthrop under his new name.'

It was just before eleven when the detective rang back. The address had turned out to be a small paper shop in Paddington. The owner agreed that he often took in mail for customers who had no fixed address. He made a charge for it. He could not remember a man called Duggan. The detective had shown him a photo of Calthrop. But the man said he had never seen him before. He also showed him the photo of Duggan from the passport form. The man said he thought he remembered the face, but could not be sure. He thought the man might have been wearing dark glasses when he came into the shop.

'Get back here quickly,' Thomas told the detective. Then he picked up the phone and asked for Lebel in Paris.

The call came half-way through the evening meeting at the Minister's office. Lebel went out to take the call. He did not come back for twenty minutes. When he did come back everyone looked up. He spoke to them for ten minutes. He ended by saying, 'So there we are. We now carry out a nation-wide hunt for a man calling himself Duggan. The British police are checking plane and cross-Channel ferry bookings. If they find him first on British soil, they pick him up. If he has left Britain they get in touch with us. If we find him in France, we arrest him. If he is in neither country, we wait until he tries to enter France, then pick him up at the border. I would be grateful, gentlemen, if you would agree to do this my way.'

They all nodded. Even Saint-Clair was silent. But inside he was angry. He was thinking to himself, Lebel takes a lot upon himself, the little upstart.

It was not until he got home, soon after midnight, that he found someone he could say this to. Jacqueline listened to him with understanding, while he got it off his chest. She stroked the back of his neck while he talked. It was not until dawn, when he was sound asleep, that she could slip away to make a short phone call.

Back in London Thomas looked at the two passport forms and photos on his desk. 'Let's run through it again,' he said to the detective sitting near him. 'Calthrop – five feet eleven tall. Check?'

'Sir,' the detective nodded.

Thomas went on, 'Duggan – six feet tall.'

'Built up shoes, sir.'

'All right,' agreed Thomas, 'it could be built up shoes. Calthrop – brown hair. That could mean anything from light brown to dark brown. Duggan also says brown, but he looks more blond to me, and Calthrop looks darker.'

'That's true, sir. But sometimes hair looks darker in photos. It depends on the lighting. And then again, he could have tinted it lighter to become Duggan.'

'All right. I'll wear that. Now, Calthrop – brown eyes: Duggan – grey eyes, so the forms say.'

'Tinted contact lenses, sir. It's a simple thing.'

Thomas looked keenly at the two photos. Calthrop was fuller in the face, a fatter man than Duggan. But to become Duggan he could have changed his looks. Men like this had to be able to live as another person – for months as a time. This was probably how Calthrop had managed to stay off every police file in the world.

But from now on he had become Duggan – tinted hair, contact lenses, built up shoes. Thomas sent the details of Duggan, with passport number and photo, to Lebel in Paris. They ought to get there next morning.

'Now it's up to them,' said the detective.

'Oh no,' Thomas said. 'We still have a lot of work to do. First thing in the morning we start checking airlines, cross-Channel ferries . . . the whole lot. We have to find where he is now as well as who he is.'

In France the next day they started checking all the records again. This time they were looking for the name Duggan. The search went on right into the night.

They found that 'Alexander Duggan' had entered France from Brussels on 22 July, and that he had gone back from Paris on 31 July. Later in the day, the police came up with a card from a Paris hotel. It showed a booking in the name of Duggan from 22 to 30 July. Lebel paid a visit to the hotel and had a chat with the owner. Then he told a plain-clothes detective to book in to the hotel himself. He was to stay there until further notice, in case Duggan turned up there again.

'This July visit,' Lebel told Caron back at the office, 'looks like a planning trip. Whatever he is going to do, it's all laid on now. He will be armed, of course. But what with? And how will he get the weapon through customs? How will he ever get anywhere near the President with it? Even women's hand-bags are suspect within twenty yards of the President.'

Caron said, 'Still, you know his new name now. And the killer doesn't know that you've found that out.'

'Yes,' Lebel agreed, 'that's my trump card at the moment. But if he gets wind of what I know and changes his name again – then I'm really in trouble.'

On Thursday morning, Thomas got a phone call from one of his team. 'Friend Duggan left London on a BEA flight to Brussels last Monday, Super.'

Thomas thought quickly. 'All right. He may have gone, but he may be back by now. Keep checking the airline bookings. I think we have lost him though. Hardly our fault, as he left London some hours before we started the search.'

'Right, sir,' the detective said.

12 The Jackal takes up painting

The Jackal got up when the sun was already high in the sky. He had a shower and put on his check suit. Soon after ten-thirty he drove the Alfa into town. He went to the post office to put a call through to Paris.

He came out twenty minutes later. He was tight-lipped and frowning hard. In a great hurry, he went to the nearest hardware shop. He bought a big tin of dark blue gloss paint and a little tin of white. He also bought some brushes and a screwdriver.

Then he drove back to the hotel and asked for his bill. While it was being made out he flicked through the pages of the hotel register. He found the entry in the name of Baroness Colette. He took note of the address of the castle where she lived.

A few minutes later the clerk heard the Alfa starting up. Then the Englishman was gone, driving away from Gap at speed.

In Lebel's office in Paris messages were coming in fast. The Brussels police rang to say that Duggan had only spent a few hours in the city. Then he had flown on to Milan. As Lebel put the phone down it rang again. This time the news was that Alexander Duggan had crossed the border into France the day before.

Lebel shouted with rage. 'Nearly thirty hours ago. And now they tell me.' Then he said to Caron, more calmly, 'Still, they said they had to sort through twenty-five thousand entry forms from all over France. At least we know one thing now. He's here in France. Ring up Superintendent Thomas in London. Thank him for all he has done. And tell him the Jackal is inside France now, and we shall handle it from here.'

As Caron finished the call to London, the phone buzzed again. It was police HQ from Lyons. Lebel listened, then looked up at Caron with a grin on his face. He put his hand over the mouth-piece. 'We've got him. He booked into a hotel at Gap for two days, starting last night.' He spoke into the phone again, 'Now listen. This is what I want you to do. . . .'

He spoke for ten minutes. As he finished there was another call. It was to report that Duggan had come into France in a hired white Alfa-Romeo, number MI 61741.

'Shall I put out an all-stations alert for the car?' Caron asked.

Lebel thought for a moment. 'No, not yet. He would most likely be picked up by a country policeman who thinks he's just looking for a stolen sports car. He'll kill anyone who tries to stop him. The important thing is that he has booked into that hotel for two nights. I want an army of police round that hotel when he gets back. The gun must be in the car somewhere. I don't want anyone to get hurt – if that's possible. Come on. If we want to be there, we must get a helicopter.'

While he was talking to Caron, the police force at Gap were moving steel road blocks into place. At two other nearby towns police armed with submachine-guns were getting into police vans.

Even in the shade of the trees, it was burning hot. It was early afternoon. The Jackal was stripped to the waist, working on the car.

After leaving Gap he had headed due west. It was downhill most of the way. He had pushed the car to the limit. He had gone on, through the mountains and then for another eighteen miles until he reached some woods. Then he thought it was time to get the Alfa off the road. He took a side road and then chose a path to the right leading into the woods.

It took him two hours to finish the car. It was the middle of the afternoon when he stood back to look at his work. The car was a deep shiny blue. Most of the paint was already dry. It was not an expert painting job. But it would get by unless looked at very closely. The two number plates had been taken off. They lay face down on the grass. On the back of each one he had painted a made-up French car number.

The car's papers did not match the blue French Alfa now. If he was stopped for a road check, he would be done for.

He reckoned that with his false name known they would soon find out where he had crossed the border into France. Then they would be looking for the car. He was days too early for the killing. He now needed a place to lie low until he was ready. That meant doing 250 miles across country. And the quickest way was in the car. It was a risk, but it had to be taken. The sooner, the better. Before every policeman in the country was looking for an Alfa with a blond Englishman at the wheel.

He fixed the new number plates on and threw away what was left of the paint, and the brushes. He put his sweater and jacket on again and started up the car. As he swept back on to the road he checked his watch. It was three-forty in the afternoon. Overhead a helicopter flew on its way east. A few minutes later he was near a village called Die. In the market square a motorcycle policeman in a black leather coat was standing, waving him to stop and pull in to the right. The Jackal's gun was still fixed to the underside of the car. For a second he was not sure whether to hit the policeman with the wing of the car and drive on, or whether to stop.

It was the policeman who made up his mind for him. As the Alfa began to slow down, the policeman looked the other way down the road. The Jackal stopped at the side of the road, watched and waited.

From the far side of the village he heard the wail of sirens. Whatever happened, it was too late to get out now. Into the village came a fleet of four Citroën police cars and six black police vans. As the traffic policeman saluted, the cars raced past the Alfa and down the road towards Gap. Through the wired windows of the vans he could see the rows of police, submachine-guns across their knees.

The policeman brought his arm down from the salute and gave the Jackal a signal to drive on.

13   Where the hell has he gone?

It was just before five o'clock when Lebel and Caron got to the hotel. Caron had a loaded submachine-gun under his coat. Everyone in the town knew by now that something was going on – except for the hotel owner. The hotel had been ringed off for over four hours.

The owner came out of his office to answer Caron's questions. Lebel was listening and his face dropped. Five minutes later the hotel was full of police in uniform. They talked to the staff, searched the bedrooms, and went through the grounds.

Lebel and Caron walked out into the drive.

'You think he has really gone, chief?' Caron asked.

Lebel nodded. 'He changed his mind some time this morning, and left. The question now is, where the hell has he gone? And does he suspect that we know who he is?'

'But how could he? It must be just pure chance.'

'Let us hope so,' Lebel said.

'All we have to go on now is the car number,' Caron said.

'Yes. That was my mistake,' Lebel said. 'I should have put out a call for the car. Get on to the Lyons police from one of the squad cars. Tell them to look for a white Alfa-Romeo, number MI 61741. Approach with care, driver believed armed. And no one is to talk to the press about it. When you have done that we'll get back to Paris.'

'You are a fool, Lebel. You had him within your grip and you let him slip.' Saint-Clair stared at Lebel.

Lebel said, 'If you look at your report, my dear Saint-Clair, you will see that we did not stand a chance. We now know that the Jackal left the hotel in a hurry just after eleven o'clock. We did not get the report about the booking until twelve-fifteen. He had an hour's start on us. Also I would remind you that the President has ordered us to keep quiet about it. We could not put out a general alert for Duggan. Another point, Duggan had booked in for two days. We do not know what made him change his mind.'

The Minister said, 'All right. We have been unlucky. But there is still the question of the car. Why was the search not started sooner?'

'I agree it was a mistake, Minister,' Lebel said, 'in the light of what has happened. But I had been told the man would still be at the hotel for the night. If he had been stopped in the car, he would probably have shot the policeman and would have been warned off. Then he would have made his escape.'

'Which is just what he has done,' Saint-Clair said.

'True, but he hasn't been warned off,' Lebel told him. 'Not as far as we know. If he checks into another hotel tonight, it will be reported. And if his car is seen, we shall also be told.'

The meeting broke up around midnight as usual.

The blue Alfa-Romeo stopped outside an all-night café at about one o'clock in the morning. The Jackal was cold and hungry. He had been driving at sixty miles an hour and the air was chilly in the mountains. He ordered some sandwiches and coffee. While he was waiting for it he went into the phone booth. He found the Baroness's name and address. He knew the name of the castle but he could not find it on his road map. But the phone number was an Egletons one, and he found the village of Egletons easily on his map. It was about fifteen miles on. He settled down to enjoy his sandwiches and coffee.

It was just before two in the morning when he passed a signpost saying 'Egletons, 6km'. He left the car in a thick wood at the side of the road, where there was a 'Private' sign. It was about half a mile along a drive off the main road. He switched off the head-lights and took the wire cutters and torch from the glove-box.

He spent an hour underneath the car. At last the steel tubes holding the gun were out of their hiding place. He put them in the suitcase, along with the Army overcoat and old clothes. He had a last look round the car to make sure he had left no clues. Then he drove it hard into the middle of a clump of bushes.

He spent another hour cutting branches from nearby bushes. He stuck them into the ground to cover up the space where he had driven the Alfa in. The car was now well hidden.

He tied a suitcase to each end of a cord and slung them over his shoulder. This left his hands free for the other two pieces of luggage. He started to walk back towards the road. It was slow going. Every few yards he stopped and put the cases down. Then he went over his tracks, sweeping away the tyre and foot marks with a tree branch.

It took another hour to get back to the road and to walk about half a mile from the drive into the forest. His suit was dirty and his arms ached. He sat down on the cases to wait. Country buses always start very early, he thought.

In fact, he was lucky. A farm cart came by at about six o'clock and he hitched a lift into Egletons. They got there well before dawn. The Jackal thanked the driver and went into a café near the station. Here he changed his suit and had a wash. Then he found a taxi and when it came he gave the driver the Baroness's address.

The Baroness was just getting out of bed. The maid had brought her a message with her morning coffee. It was from her husband to say he would be staying in Paris for a while 'on business'.

She stood in front of the long mirror. 'On business,' she thought angrily. 'Well, two can play at that game.' She shook her long black hair so that a strand lay across her breast. 'Not bad,' she thought, looking at her figure in the mirror. She wished she had stayed on at the hotel in Gap. She could have had a good time with that Englishman.

There was a clatter of an old car stopping in the courtyard. She went to the window. There was an old taxi there and two men were takings things out of the boot. One of the men got into the driving seat and drove off. She gave a start of surprise. There were three suitcases and a hand-grip standing on the drive. Beside them stood a tall man with blond hair.

'You beautiful man,' she said under her breath. 'You followed me.'

She dressed quickly.

Later that evening, the Jackal lay on the bed, staring up at the gold ceiling of the bedroom. He had just eaten a splendid meal, had a bath and was resting. He was planning in his mind the job he had to do in Paris and what he would do until then. In a week he would have to move.

The door opened and Colette came in. She wore a thin housecoat tied at the neck with ribbon. The Jackal propped himself up on one elbow as she came over to the bed. Then he reached up and undid the ribbon. He slid the housecoat off her shoulders. It slid to the floor without a sound.

14   Waiting for what?

For three days the trail went cold. The evening meetings at the Minister's office were getting nowhere. Some of them thought the Jackal must have left France by now. Only Lebel still thought that the killer was still lying low, biding his time.

'Waiting for what?' shouted Saint-Clair on the third evening. 'The only thing he can be waiting for is a chance to make a dash for the border. The moment he breaks cover we have got him.'

There were nods from the others round the table. Lebel shook his head. He was very tired from lack of sleep. He knew that if he was wrong he was finished. Some of the men round the table would see to that. His long career in the police force would be over. Unless . . . unless he could find the killer and stop him. Only then would they have to admit that he had been right.

'Waiting for I don't know what,' Lebel said. 'But he is waiting for something, for some special day. I do not think that we have heard the last of the Jackal yet.'

On the morning of 20 August a gamekeeper was looking for a wounded pigeon that had fallen into a clump of bushes. In the middle of the clump he found the bird on the seat of an open sports car.

At first he thought that it must have been parked there by a loving couple. Then he saw that some of the branches that hid the car were not growing, but just stuck into the ground.

From the bird droppings on the car, he reckoned it had been there for some days. He would tell the local policeman when he went into the village later that morning.

It was nearly noon when the village policeman sent the report in. Was it a white car? he was asked. No, it was a blue car. The police station at the nearest town promised to send a truck to tow it away.

The truck did not come until nearly four that afternoon. The car was towed to the police station and the staff began to check it over. It was nearly five o'clock when one of them noticed that the paintwork was badly done. He took a screwdriver and scratched at one of the wings. Under the blue was a streak of white. Puzzled, he looked at the number plates. They seemed to have been put on the wrong way round. A few minutes later the front number plate was lying on the ground. He turned it over. In white lettering he read MI 61741. The policeman ran to the phone.

Lebel got the news just before six. He suddenly sat up and said into the phone, 'Right. Listen. This is important. I can't say why. Get a team down there now. The best you can get, and as many men as you can get. Start from the spot where the car was found. Work outwards from there. Ask at every farm-house, every village shop and café, every hotel, and stop any drivers on the road. You are looking for a tall, blond Englishman who speaks good French. He was carrying three suitcases and a hand-grip.'

'Your men must ask where he was, where he went, what he bought. And the Press must be kept out at all costs. Play it down. If you find the man hiding somewhere, don't go near him. Just surround him and keep him there. I'll be down as soon as I can.'

Lebel put the phone down and turned to Caron.

'Get on to the Minister. Ask him to change the evening meeting to eight o'clock. Then get the helicopter again.'

The police vans set up their HQ in the village square, near to the spot where the car was found. The sun was just setting. They were to work through the night and they had to cover a five-mile square. People were more likely to be at home after dark.

Before midnight two of the policemen were talking to a farmer at his cottage door. It was two miles from where the car was found. The farmer would not ask the policemen in.

'Come on, you drive along that road pretty often. Did you drive to Egletons on Friday morning?'

The farmer looked at them in an unfriendly way.

'I might have done,' he said.

'Did you see a man – a blond man – tall, carrying three suit-cases and a hand-grip?'

'I saw nothing.'

It went on for twenty minutes. At last they went. One of the detectives made some notes on his pad. The farmer watched them until they were back on the road. Then he slammed the door and got back into bed with his wife.

'That was about the chap you gave a lift to, wasn't it?' she asked. 'What do they want with him?'

'Don't know. But no one will ever say I gave another chap away to *them*. Dirty pigs. Good luck to you wherever you are, mate.'

Lebel faced the meeting and put down his papers. 'As soon as this meeting is over, gentlemen, I am going down to head the search myself.'

There was a long silence.

Someone asked, 'What do you make of this?'

Lebel said, 'Two things. We know he must have bought paint to cover the car. He may have bought it in Gap. If so, then he was tipped off. Either he rang somebody, or somebody rang him. It could have been from France or from London. It must have been someone who told him that the name Duggan was known to the police. So he got out, and fast.'

'Are you really saying there is a leak from within this room?' the Minister asked.

'I can't say that, sir. It might be one of the switchboard girls. It could be that one of them is a secret OAS agent. But one thing seems to be clear. He has been warned off, but he still means to carry on with the job.'

The Minister got up, 'We must not keep you, Lebel. Find him. Find him tonight. Kill him if you have to. Those are my orders, in the name of the President.'

An hour later Lebel's helicopter was on its way.

'Cheeky bastard. How dare he take all this on himself,' Saint-Clair told his girlfriend. 'I shall mention it in my next report, of course. He thinks he knows it all.'

Jacqueline let the thin straps of her nightdress fall from her shoulders. She took her lover's head and pulled him towards her.

'Tell me all about it, darling,' she said softly.

15 Murder again

The morning of 21 August was bright and clear. The Jackal stood at the window in the castle, making his daily phone call to Paris. He had left Colette asleep upstairs.

When he was through to Paris he began as usual, 'Jackal here.'

'Valmy here,' came the reply. 'Things have started to move again. They have found the car.'

He listened for another two minutes, asking a question now and then. With a final 'thank you' he put the phone down. What he had just heard made him think for a moment. He had to change his plans now, whether he liked it or not. He had wanted to stay on at the castle for another two days. But now, the sooner he left the better. There was something else about the phone call that troubled him. There had been a soft click on the line when he picked up the phone. There was another phone in the bedroom. But surely, Colette was still asleep. He ran up the stairs and burst into the bedroom.

The phone was back on its rest. The wardrobe was open and the three suitcases lay about the floor. They were all open. His keys lay on the floor, too. Colette, on her knees, looked up, her eyes wide. Around her lay a set of slim steel tubes, all open. She held something in her hands. Something she had been looking at in horror when he burst in. It was the barrel and breech of the gun.

For several seconds neither of them spoke.

Then the Jackal said, 'You were listening.'

'I . . . wondered who you were phoning each morning,' she said.

'I thought you were asleep.'

'No. I always wake when you get out of bed. This . . . thing – it's a gun. A killer's gun.'

He looked down at her. For the first time she saw in his eyes a cold hard look. It was like a machine staring down at her.

'You want to kill him,' she said. 'You are one of them, the OAS. You want to use this to kill the President.'

The Jackal said nothing. She made a rush for the door. He caught her easily and threw her back on to the bed. As she hit the bed her mouth opened to scream. The back-handed blow across the side of her neck cut off the scream. Then his left hand was caught in her hair. He dragged her face down over the edge of the bed. She saw the pattern on the carpet. Then a forehand chop from the edge of his hand came down on the back of her neck.

The Jackal went to the door and listened. No sound came from below. He packed up the parts of the rifle in their tubes and put them in the suitcase. Then he locked the cases.

He spent five minutes washing and shaving. Then he combed his hair upwards and snipped off the last two inches. He got out the hair dye and brushed it into his hair. He then combed it into the style shown in the Danish parson's passport photo. He propped the photo up on the bathroom shelf, so that he would get it just right. Last of all, he slipped in the blue-tinted contact lenses.

He wiped every trace of the hair tint off the wash-basin. He went back to the bedroom, stepping over the naked body on the floor. He dressed in the underwear that he had bought in Denmark. Round his neck he fixed the black bib front and parson's dog collar. He put on the black suit and walking shoes. He put the gold-rimmed glasses into his top pocket. His washing kit went into the hand-grip. Into the inside pocket of his suit he put the parson's passport and a bundle of money.

It was nearly eight when he had finished. At that moment the maid knocked on the door. She had brought the Baroness's cup of coffee.

'Your coffee is here, madam,' she said.

The Jackal called out in a sleepy voice, 'Leave it there. We'll pick it up when we are ready.'

The maid's mouth dropped open. Shocking. Whatever were things coming to . . . and in the master's bedroom, too. She went downstairs, leaving the coffee tray outside the bedroom door. She did not hear the soft thud as the cases dropped from the bedroom window on to the flower-bed below. Nor did she hear as the Jackal softly locked the bedroom door from the inside. He lifted Colette's limp body on to the bed and placed it in a natural sleeping position. Then the grey-haired man dropped from the window to the lawn below.

She did hear the roar of the Baroness's car as it swung into the drive. 'Now what is that young lady up to?' she thought as she went back upstairs. The coffee tray was still there. The coffee was still warm. She knocked several times. There was no reply. She tried the door. It was locked. She knocked on the gentleman's bedroom door. Nobody would answer her.

16   A single ticket to Paris

Lebel took the helicopter back to Paris soon after breakfast time. He had traced the Jackal to a café in Egletons where he had had a snack and picked up a taxi. In the meantime he had ordered road blocks to be set up in a ring round Egletons.

By this time the Jackal was speeding through the mountains, heading south in Colette's Renault. He reckoned that the police must have got to Egletons by dawn. The café barman would talk. So would the taxi driver. They would be at the castle by the afternoon.

But even then they would be looking for a blond Englishman. He had taken good care that no one had seen him as a grey-haired parson. All the same, it was going to be a close thing.

He speeded up the car and came out on to a road about nine miles south-west of Egletons. As he vanished round a bend, a small convoy came rushing along from Egletons. It was a police squad car and two closed vans. They stopped in the middle of the road and six policemen started to put up a steel road block.

'What do you mean, he's out?' the detective shouted to the weeping wife of the taxi driver. 'Where did he go to?'

'I don't know, sir. I don't know. He waits every morning at the station when the morning train comes in. If he does not pick up a fare there or at the café, he comes back here and gets on with some repair work.'

'Did he pick anybody up on Friday morning?'

'He did say that he had picked someone up in Egletons. He never said where he took them. He doesn't talk to me much.'

The detective patted her on the shoulder. 'All right, madam. Don't upset yourself. We'll wait until he gets back.'

He turned to one of the policemen. 'Get a man to the station, another to the café. You know the number of that taxi. The moment he shows up I want to see him.'

In a valley, many miles away, the Jackal got rid of one of the suitcases. It had all his English clothes in it, and the passport of Alexander Duggan. It had served him well. Then he went to the nearest town and found the railway station. He parked the car three streets away and carried his two suitcases and hand-grip to the booking office.

'A single ticket to Paris, please, second class,' he said. He had nearly an hour to wait. The next train was at eleven-fifty. He went to the barrier. His ticket was clipped and he walked through. Standing in his way was a man in a blue uniform.

'Your papers, please,' the policeman said. He carried a submachine-gun over his shoulder. The Jackal put down his luggage and showed his Danish passport. The policeman looked through it, not understanding a word.

'You are Danish?' he asked.

'Pardon,' the Jackal said, pretending not to understand.

'You . . . Danish,' the man tapped the passport.

The Jackal grinned and nodded, 'Danske . . . ja, ja,' he said.

The man handed back his passport and made a sign to the 'parson' to carry on to the platform for the Paris train. Then, without any more interest, he stepped forward to stop the next person coming through the ticket barrier.

It was not until about one o'clock that the Baroness's maid was able to tell her tale to her husband. He had been at the market all morning. He took the matter in hand at once.

'I shall climb up to the window and look in,' he said. He had trouble with the ladder to start with. But at last he got it propped up under the window. He went up and looked through the bedroom window. He was down again in a few seconds.

'The Baroness is fast asleep,' he told his wife.

'But she never sleeps this late,' she said.

'Well, she is doing today. We must not disturb her,' he said.

They had lunch and the husband went out to work in the garden. It was not until four o'clock that the maid got her husband to go up the ladder again.

'You must go and look again,' she said. 'It's not natural for anyone to sleep right through the day. She may be ill.'

He went up the ladder, pushed the window open and stepped inside. His wife waited down below in the garden. After a few minutes he popped his head out of the window and called down to her, 'Madam seems to be dead.' He was just going to climb down again when his wife shouted, 'Open the bedroom door from the inside, and I'll come up.'

Together they peered over the edge of the sheet at the eyes of their mistress. They were open and staring.

The maid said, 'Hurry down to the village and fetch the doctor.' Her husband got out his bike and was soon off as fast as his legs would pedal.

It was past four-thirty when the doctor's car drew up outside the castle. He went up and looked at the body on the bed. The maid and her husband were standing in the doorway.

'Madam is dead,' he said. 'Her neck has been broken. We must get the police.'

17 The parson is in Paris

The phone rang in Lebel's office. It was the detective in charge of the team working from the place where the Alfa had been found.

99

'Nothing to report, so far,' he told Lebel. 'We have road blocks up on every road and every track. He must be inside the square somewhere, unless he moved far away fast. That blasted taxi driver who drove him out of Egletons on Friday morning hasn't shown up yet. I've got men out looking for him. . . . Hold it a minute, there's another report just coming in from one of the team.'

Lebel waited. He could hear the detective talking to someone else. Then he came back on the line.

'There has been a murder, chief,' he said.

'Where?' Lebel asked with new interest.

'At a castle nearby. The report has just come in from the village policeman.'

'Who is the victim?' Lebel shouted.

'A woman. Hold on a moment. . . . A Baroness, Colette somebody or other.'

Lebel went pale. 'It's him. Has he got away from the castle?'

'Yes,' the detective told him. 'He drove away this morning in the dead woman's car. A small Renault. The servants found her body – but not until this afternoon. They thought she was asleep at first.'

'Have you got the car number?' Lebel said.

'Yes.'

'Then put out a general alert. There's no need to keep it secret any more. It's a straight murder hunt now.'

Lebel hung up. 'Dear God,' he said to himself, 'I'm getting slow in my old age. The Baroness's name was on the hotel list the night the Jackal was there.'

The Renault was found in a back street by a policeman on the beat. It was five past eight when Lebel got to hear about it. The detective told him, 'It was found about five hundred metres from the railway station.'

Lebel said, 'Have you got a rail timetable there?'

'Yes,' the detective told him.

'Quick. What was the time of the morning train from there to Paris? And what time is it due in Paris? Hurry, for God's sake, hurry.'

'There are only two trains a day from there to Paris,' the detective said. 'The morning train left at eleven-fifty and is due in Paris at . . . here we are . . . ten past eight.'

Lebel left the phone hanging and was half-way out of the office, yelling at Caron to follow him.

The express train steamed into Paris right on time at ten past eight. It had hardly stopped when the doors were flung open and the people spilled out. Among them was a tall parson with grey hair. He was one of the first at the taxi rank. He had two cases and a hand-grip. He got into the next taxi that came along.

The driver pushed the meter over and drove away from the station. As the taxi reached the street there was a wailing sound. Three squad cars and two Black Marias swept into the station yard.

'The bastards are very busy tonight,' the taxi driver said. 'Where to, sir?'

The parson pretended to frown at the swear word, then gave the address of a small hotel.

Lebel was back in his office at nine o'clock. It was the chief detective again who phoned in.

'We have taken fingerprints from the car, and from the bedroom at the castle. Hundreds of sets, all matching.'

Lebel said, 'Get them up here as fast as you can.'

'Right, will do.'

'You can stand your boys down now. He's in Paris now. We will have to handle it from here. Thanks for all your work.'

The detective said, 'You are sure it's the Danish parson, are you?'

'It's him all right. He got rid of one of the suitcases somewhere. Try the river valleys and woods. But the other three pieces of luggage match. It's him all right.' He hung up.

'A parson this time,' Lebel said bitterly to Caron. 'A Danish parson. We don't know the name. The policeman at the station couldn't remember the name on the passport. One thing I can tell you, Caron. I'm getting too old for this game – too old and too slow. Get my car ready, will you? Time for the meeting at the Minister's office. They will all be out for my blood tonight.'

The evening meeting was tense. They all listened to a long report of the trail from the forest to Egletons; the missing taxi driver; the murder in the castle; the tall grey-haired parson getting the train to Paris.

Saint-Clair said coldly, 'So, the killer is now in Paris, with a new name and a new face. You seem to have failed us once again, my dear Lebel.'

'Let us save the brick-bats for later,' said the Minister. 'How many Danes are there in Paris?'

'Probably several hundred, Minister,' Lebel told him.

The Minister said, 'I will have every hotel checked at midnight, two o'clock and four o'clock in the morning. He will be forced to put "parson" on the booking form. So we shall find him.'

The meeting began to feel more hopeful. The Minister went on, 'At this point, there is only one thing left to do. I shall ask to see the President and beg him to cancel all public duties until this killer is found.'

'The thing that gets me,' said Lebel to Caron later, 'is that they keep on thinking it's just his good luck, and that we are stupid. Well, he has had good luck, but he is also very clever. We have had bad luck, and we've made mistakes. But there's something else. Twice we have missed him by only hours. Each time it has been the day after I have told the evening meeting we have him in the bag. I think I'm going to use my powers and set up a bit of wire-tapping.'

Part Three
The Kill

1 A visit to Valmy

Lebel had had a bad night. It was half past one when Caron woke him, and he had only just got to sleep.

'Chief, I'm sorry about this. But I've had an idea. This Jackal, he has a Danish passport, right?'

Lebel shook himself awake. 'Go on.'

'Well, where did he get it from? As he had to tint his hair to match the photo, it looks as though he must have stolen it.'

'Yes, go on.'

'Well, apart from his trip to Paris in July, he has been based in London. So the chances are that he stole it in Paris or London. What would a Dane do if his passport was stolen? He would go to the Consul.'

Lebel got up. 'Sometimes, my dear Caron, I think you will go far. Get me Superintendent Thomas on the phone. He will be at home – you've got the number, it's in Surrey. After that be ready to get me the Danish Consul in Paris.'

Lebel was nearly an hour on the phone. By then he had begged both men to leave their beds and go back to their offices.

At six a call came from the engineers who had been told to fix up the wire-tapping. They were on to something. They were recording it now.

Lebel and Caron jumped into the car and rushed down to police HQ. The engineers put on a tape-recording for them. It started with a loud click. Then came the noise of seven numbers on the dial. Then there was the buzz of a phone ringing, and another click as the phone was lifted at the other end.

A husky voice said, 'Hello.'

A woman's voice next. 'Jacqueline here.'

'Valmy here,' the man said.

Jacqueline said quickly, 'They know he is a Danish parson. They are checking the hotels. Three checks, one at midnight, then at two o'clock and four o'clock.'

The man just said, 'Thank you,' and hung up.

Lebel looked at the slowly turning tape. 'Do you know the number she rang?' he asked.

'Yes. We work it out from the time it takes the dial to spin back to zero,' one of the engineers said.

'Have you found out the address?'

The man passed him a slip of paper.

Lebel said, 'Come on, Caron. We are going to call on Mr Valmy.'

The knock came at seven o'clock in the morning. The schoolmaster was making himself a cup of tea. He was still in his dressing-gown. When he opened the front door four men were facing him. He knew who they were without being told. The two in uniform looked as though they were going to grab him. But the small, mild-looking plain-clothes man told them, 'Stay where you are.'

'We tapped the phone,' the little man said quietly. 'You are Valmy.' The schoolmaster's face was a blank. He stepped back and let them enter the room. 'May I get dressed?' he asked.

'Yes, of course.'

It took him only a few minutes. 'Take him down to the car,' the little man said.

When the others had left, the little man stayed behind in Valmy's flat. He looked through the papers on the table, but they were only exam papers. The schoolmaster must have been marking them. He must have done all his work from the flat. He would have to be there all day in case the Jackal phoned in. At ten past seven the phone began to ring.

Lebel looked at it for several seconds, then he picked it up. 'Hello,' he said, trying to make his voice sound husky.

The voice on the other end was flat. 'Jackal here.'

Lebel thought quickly. 'Valmy here,' he said. There was a pause.

'What's new?' the Jackal said.

'Nothing. They lost the trail.' There was sweat on Lebel's face. It was vital the Jackal should stay where he was for a few hours more. There was a click and the phone went dead. Lebel put it down and ran downstairs to the car.

'Back to the office,' he yelled at the driver.

In the phone booth of a small hotel the Jackal looked puzzled. How could they have lost the trail? This Lebel fellow was no fool. They must have found the taxi driver in Egletons by now. They must have found the body at the castle. They must have found the Renault. . . .

He rushed out of the phone booth and across the hotel lobby.

'My bill, if you please,' he told the clerk at the desk. 'I shall be down in five minutes.'

Soon after Lebel got back to his office there was a phone call. It was from Superintendent Thomas in England. 'Sorry to have been so long,' Thomas said. 'It took ages to wake the Danish Consul and get him to go back to the office. You were quite right. On 14 July a Danish parson reported the loss of his passport. Name of Jensen. Six feet tall, blue eyes, grey hair.'

'That's the one. Thank you.' Lebel put the phone down. To Caron he said, 'Get me police HQ.'

The four police vans got to the hotel at eight-thirty. The police turned room 37 over until it looked as if a bomb had hit it.

'I'm sorry,' the owner told them. 'Parson Jensen checked out an hour ago.'

2 Freedom day

The Jackal had taken a taxi back to the station – the same station he had come into the evening before. He reckoned that the manhunt would be on somewhere else now. He left the suitcase with the gun in it at the left-luggage office. The Army greatcoat and shabby clothes were also in the case. He kept with him the case that held the clothes and papers of the American student, and the hand-grip with the make-up in it. He was still dressed in the black suit, but had put a polo-neck sweater over the parson's dog collar. Taking the case and the grip, he checked into a shabby little hotel round the corner from the station. The clerk gave him a booking card to fill in. The rules said that the booking card had to be checked against the passport. But the clerk was too lazy to do this. As a result, the card was not even filled in with the name of Jensen.

Once up in his room, the Jackal set to work on his face and hair. He washed out the grey tint and rinsed his hair with the chestnut brown tint of Marty Schulberg. He left the blue contact lenses in but put on the heavy-rimmed glasses. He dressed now in the jeans, T-shirt, windcheater and sneakers of the American college boy.

By mid-morning he was ready to move. He had the American passport and a bundle of notes in his pockets. He left the case with the parson's clothes in the wardrobe. He left by the fire-escape. A few minutes later he was back at the railway station. He left the hand-grip at the left-luggage office. He put the ticket for it in his back pocket, along with the ticket for the suitcase. He took a taxi and vanished into the crowds on the Left Bank of Paris.

Lebel was on the phone again to Thomas in London. What he was asking for made Thomas groan. But he said he would do everything he could to help. When he put the phone down, Thomas sent for one of his team.

'The French have been back on,' he told him. 'It seems they have missed the Jackal again. Now he's somewhere in the middle of Paris and Lebel thinks he may have yet another name and face. He wants us to ring every Consul office in London. He wants a list of passports reported lost or stolen from any visitors from overseas. He wants us to check back to the first of July. Everybody above five feet eight tall is suspect Get to work.'

The daily meeting at the Ministry in Paris had been brought forward to two in the afternoon. Lebel gave his report.

'Blast the man,' said the Minister. 'He has the luck of the devil.'

'No, Minister. It's not just luck,' Lebel said. 'He has been tipped off about our steps at every stage. Three times we have been within hours of catching him. Each time he was tipped off after I had made my report to this meeting.'

There was a stunned silence round the table.

The Minister said, 'I remember, Lebel, that you have hinted at this before. Can you prove it?'

Lebel lifted a small tape-recorder on to the table. He pressed the start button. When the tape had ended the whole room was silent. Saint-Clair had gone deathly white as the truth hit him.

'Whose voice was that woman's?' the Minister asked at last.

Lebel said nothing. Everyone froze. Saint-Clair got up very slowly. All eyes turned on him.

'I regret to have to tell you, Minister . . . that it was the voice of . . . a friend of mine. She is staying with me at the present time. I must, of course, give in my notice. Excuse me.'

He left the room. The Minister spoke in a quiet voice. 'Go on with your report, please, Lebel.'

Lebel told them that in London Superintendent Thomas was checking every missing or stolen passport. 'I hope to have a short list by this evening,' he told them. 'There will probably only be one or two that could possibly fit the Jackal. With luck I should have photos of them by noon tomorrow.'

'For my part,' the Minister said, 'I can report on my visit to the President. He has refused point-blank to change an item of his programme in the interests of his own safety. But the order to keep it all secret can now be lifted. As soon as Lebel is quite sure of the Jackal's new name and face, we will fill the Press in. We will give them the name and the photo as part of the murder-in-the-castle story. It can also go out on radio and television. Apart from that, the moment we get a name, every policeman in Paris will be stopping people in the street to check their papers. As regards the President himself, I want a full list of every move he intends to take from now on.'

The Minister looked at Bouvier then and said, 'As for the Crime Squad, they have a lot of informers in their pay. I want them all told to keep an eye open for this man. Right?'

Bouvier nodded. He had seen a few manhunts in his time, but this was really big. The moment Lebel gave them a name and a passport number, there would be a hundred thousand men hunting the streets, hotels and bars for one man.

'Well, that's it then,' the Minister said. 'All we want from you now, Lebel, is one name and one photo. After that I give the Jackal six hours.'

'In fact, we have three days, Minister,' Lebel said. Everyone looked at him.

'How do you know that?' the Minister asked.

'I should have thought of it before,' Lebel said. 'The Jackal has picked his day. Otherwise, when he left Gap why did he spend a week killing time? He knows when he is going to strike. What is Sunday, 25 August?'

There was a sigh round the table like wind blowing through corn.

'Of course,' the Minister said. 'Freedom Day.'

'Just so,' Lebel said. 'He knows there is one day in the year that the President will never spend anywhere but here in Paris. It is, so to speak, his great day. That is what the killer has been waiting for.'

'In that case,' the Minister said, 'we have got him. There

is no corner of Paris where he can hide from us. Lebel, get us that man's name.'

Lebel got up and went to the door.

'Oh, there is one thing,' the Minister called after him. 'How did you know to tap Saint-Clair's phone?'

Lebel turned back. 'I didn't,' he said. 'I tapped all your phones. Good day, gentlemen.'

3   One more death

It was eight o'clock when Thomas came through on the phone from London. Eight men had lost their passports in London during the last fifty days – that is, eight men who were about the same height as the Jackal. He gave Lebel the names and passport numbers and what the men looked like.

'Now who can we cross out?' Lebel said to Caron when he had put the phone down. 'Three lost their passports when we know the Jackal was not in London. Of the others, one is too tall, six feet six; one is so very fat that the Jackal would have to wear so much padding he could hardly walk; one is too old, over seventy.'

'That only leaves two,' Caron said.

'Well, one comes from Norway, the other from America,' Lebel said. 'But there are two things against the one from Norway. For one thing he is blond. I don't think the Jackal would go back to his own colour at this stage. The other thing is that he told the Consul he feels sure he dropped his passport in the river from a boat. On the other hand, the American said that his hand-grip with his passport in it was stolen while he was at the airport. Get Thomas to send me everything he can find about the American.'

There was a second meeting at the Ministry that evening. An hour before they met, details of Marty Schulberg had been sent out to every police force. The photo would reach them by the morning, in time for the early newspapers.

The Minister got up. 'Gentlemen, we have been very lucky indeed to have the services of Mr Lebel. In spite of three changes of name and face, and in spite of having had our secrets betrayed, he has found out who our man is. We owe him our thanks.' There were nods from the others round the table as the Minister went on. 'But from now on the task must rest with us. We have a name and we will soon have a picture. We should have our man within hours.' He turned to Lebel. 'We shall not be needing your expert help in the hours to come. Your task is done, and well done. Thank you.'

Lebel got up. He nodded at the men round the table. They smiled back at him. He turned and left the room.

For the first time in ten days he went home to bed – and to some strong words from his wife. As he fell asleep the clock struck midnight, and it was now 23 August.

The bright idea had come to the Jackal during the afternoon. He was sitting drinking beer outside a café. He watched two men walking down the street. He paid for his beer and left. A hundred yards down the street he found what he was looking for. It was a beauty salon. He went in and bought a few things.

Just before midnight, when Lebel was getting into his own bed, the Jackal walked into a bar. The barman stared hard at him. All talk stopped at the tables near the door as the tall young man walked up to the bar. The hush spread down the room and everyone had a good look at the new man. He could hear some laughs and a whisper or two behind him. He sat down on a high stool at the bar.

The barman came over to get a better look. His lips were painted and he smiled as he said, 'Good evening, sir.'

'Bring me a Scotch,' the Jackal said.

The barman went off to get the drink and thought to himself that there was going to be quite a scene tonight. This new boy was going to cause a stir.

The man next to the Jackal at the bar turned towards him. His hair had tinted gold streaks in it. His eyes and his lips were made-up.

'Are you going to have a drink with me?'

The Jackal shook his head. The man with the make-up shrugged and turned back to his friend.

The Jackal made his move soon after. A man at the back of the room had been staring at him for some time. He was alone at a table. The Jackal slid off his stool and walked slowly over.

'Would you let me sit here?' he asked.

The other man, who was middle-aged and rather smart, was delighted. They left the bar together about one o'clock in the morning. The Jackal had told his new friend that he was an American student, down on his luck. He had nowhere to stay.

The man, who was called Jules, had wasted no time in inviting the Jackal to stay at his flat. He lived alone. He would be delighted if young Marty would stay with him. Just before they left the bar, the Jackal slipped into the cloakroom. He came out a few minutes later with his face made-up with lipstick and thick eye shadow.

Outside in the street, Jules said, 'I don't like you in that stuff. You are a good-looking young man. You don't need all that.'

'Sorry, Jules,' the Jackal said. 'I thought you would like it. I'll wipe it all off when we get to your flat.'

Jules led the way to his big car. He drove his new friend to the station first so that he could collect his bags from the left-luggage.

As they drove on to the flat a policeman stepped into the road and waved them down. The Jackal wound the window down as the policeman came to the car. The policeman drew back in horror when he saw their faces.

'Oh, my God. Where are you two going?'

The Jackal said, 'Where do you think, duckie?'

The policeman said, 'You make me feel sick, your sort. Move on.'

'You should have asked to see their papers,' the policeman's mate said.

'Oh, come on,' the first policeman said. 'We are looking for a chap who made love to a Baroness and then did her in, not a couple of men like that.'

Jules and the Jackal were inside the flat by two o'clock. The Jackal insisted on sleeping on the sofa in the living room.

In the night the Jackal checked the fridge in the kitchen. There was enough food for one person for three days. He and Jules had a late breakfast and spent the rest of the morning talking. The Jackal put the television on at mid-day to see the news.

The first thing on was about the hunt for the killer of the Baroness. Jules cried out in horror. 'Ooh, I can't stand murders.'

The next second the screen was filled with the face of a young man with chestnut brown hair and heavy-rimmed glasses. The newsman said the wanted man was an American student called Marty Schulberg. Would anybody having seen this man. . . .

Jules was sitting on the sofa. He turned round and looked up at the Jackal. But the eyes that were looking down into his were no longer friendly. They were cold and grey as the steel fingers closed round his throat. . . .

A few minutes later the door of the hall cupboard closed on the staring, twisted face of Jules. The Jackal took a magazine from the rack in the living room, lit a cigarette, and settled down to wait for two days.

4 A day in the life of a President

During those two days Paris was searched as it had never been searched before. Every hotel was visited and the guest-list checked; every doss-house, bar, café and night-club was checked. Plain-clothes men were everywhere showing the photo of the wanted man to waiters, barmen and café owners. The house of every known OAS man was raided and turned over.

Thousands of people in the streets, in taxis and on buses were stopped and their papers checked. Road blocks were set up on all the main roads into Paris. French families who had students from abroad staying with them were visited and warned.

On the evening of 24 August, Lebel was called on the phone. He had spent his Saturday afternoon working in the garden of his home. It was the Minister's office. He was told to report in. A car would come for him at six.

The Minister looked as though he hadn't slept for days. 'We can't find him,' he said shortly. 'He has disappeared. The OAS don't know where he is, any more than we do. What do you think?'

'He is here somewhere. I know that,' Lebel said. 'What's going to happen about tomorrow?'

'The President won't have anything changed. I spoke to him this morning. So tomorrow stays the same as planned. He will light the flame at the grave of the Unknown Soldier. High Mass in Notre Dame at eleven. Back to the Palace for lunch. In the afternoon he presents medals to ten old soldiers. That's at four o'clock on the square in front of the old station at the end of the Rue de Rennes. He chose the place himself.'

'What about crowd control?' Lebel asked.

'The crowds are to be kept further back than usual,' the Minister told him. 'Steel barriers are to go up several hours before each event. Then the area inside the barriers will be searched from top to bottom. That includes the sewers. Every house and flat will be searched. There will be watchers with guns on every roof-top nearby.

'We have gone to great lengths this time. Even the priests taking part in the Mass will be searched. The police are having special badges given out tomorrow at dawn, in case he tries to get through as a policeman. All press passes are going to be changed at dawn tomorrow, and the passes for people taking part in the events. Everyone who comes within two hundred metres of the President will be searched.

'We have spent the last day putting bullet-proof windows into the President's car. Even the President doesn't know about that. He would be hopping mad. So keep that to yourself. Well, have you any more ideas?'

Lebel thought for a moment. 'I don't think that he will risk getting killed himself. He's doing it for the money. He wants to live to spend it. If he was not cock-sure about his chances of pulling it off, he would have turned back before now. So he must have something up his sleeve.'

Lebel got up and paced up and down the room. 'He must have hit on some idea that nobody has thought of before. It has to be a time bomb, or a gun. But a bomb could be found and that would ruin the whole thing. So it's a gun. That was why he had to enter France by car.'

'But how can he get a gun through the barriers?' the Minister cried.

Lebel stood still and faced the Minister. 'I don't know. But *he* thinks he can, and he has not failed yet. One thing is sure, Minister. Wherever he is, he must come out tomorrow. So may I just wander round at each of the public events and see if I can spot him? It's the only thing left to do.'

The Minister frowned. He had hoped for some brain-wave from Lebel.

'Of course,' he said coldly. 'Please do just that.'

Later that evening the Jackal got ready in Jules's bedroom. On the bed were a pair of scruffy black shoes, grey socks, old trousers and shirt and a long Army overcoat. The coat had a row of medals on it. There was also the black beret of the old soldier André Martin and the false papers, forged in Brussels.

Beside these he laid the steel tubes with the rifle parts in them. There was also a black rubber stud with five explosive bullets stuffed inside it. He took two of the bullets out and prised the noses off them carefully. He slid out of each a small piece of cordite. He threw the shells, now useless, into the bin. He still had three bullets left, and that would be enough.

He had not shaved for two days, and his chin was covered with stubble. He would shave this off badly with a cut-throat razor. On the bathroom shelf were the after-shave bottles with the hair tint in. He had already washed out the chestnut brown tint of Marty Schulberg. Sitting in front of the bathroom mirror, he cut his hair shorter and shorter. Tufts stuck up from the top of his head in a messy brush-cut. Then he cooked himself some eggs and watched the television until it was time for bed.

Sunday, 25 August 1963, was a scorching hot day. Paris was on holiday to mark its being freed from the Germans nineteen years before. Most of the people hardly got a sight of the President as he walked through solid ranks of guards and policemen. His four personal bodyguards were also close at hand. Each one carried a submachine-gun under his left arm. They walked with hands half-open, ready to sweep the gun out at the first hint of trouble.

But there was none. The event at the grave of the Unknown Soldier went off as planned. It was the same at the Mass at Notre Dame. In the organ loft two men with rifles watched the people down below. Nothing happened.

That morning the Jackal was somewhere else.

5   Poor old man

Peter Valremy was fed up. He was hot, his shirt was sticking to his back. The strap of his gun was rubbing his shoulder sore. He was hungry, and it was just on lunch-time. He knew he was going to miss lunch today. He was beginning to wish he had never joined the CRS anti-riot squad. He had been on duty for hours now.

No one had told him about life in the barracks. It was more like life in prison. Nor had they told him about the drill, or the hours of waiting on street corners. It was either bitter cold or blazing hot. He seemed to spend his time waiting for the Great Catch that never came.

And now, Paris. It was his first trip to the big city. He had thought he might see some of the sights. Not a hope. Just the orders from the officer, 'See that crowd barrier, Valremy? Well, stand by it, watch it, see it doesn't move and don't let a soul through unless they have a pass. Yours is an important job, my lad.'

Important indeed! Mind you, they had gone a bit mad over this Freedom Day. They had brought in men from ten different city forces.

Valremy turned round and looked back up the Rue de Rennes. The barrier stretched across the street from one side to the other. At the end was the old railway station with the square in front. That was where the old soldiers would get their medals from the President. In the distance he could see men marking out the spots where the old soldiers had to stand. Three hours to go yet. God, would it never end?

Along the barriers, the first people were starting to gather. Fancy waiting in this heat, he thought. Waiting for hours just to see a lot of heads 300 metres away. They would never even see the President in the middle of that lot. Still they always came when he was about.

There were over a hundred people waiting at the barriers

when he saw the old man. He was hobbling down the street looking as though he was never going to make another half-mile. His face was wet with sweat and his long overcoat fell below his knees. There was a row of medals clinking on his coat. Some of the people cast him looks full of pity. These old chaps always kept their medals, Valremy thought to himself, as though they were the only thing they had left in life. Well, maybe it *was* the only thing left for some of them. It probably was for this old man, with one of his legs shot off. Fancy having to spend the rest of your days limping about with one leg, propping yourself up on a crutch. The old man hobbled up to him.

'Can I go through?' he asked timidly.

'Come on, Dad. Let's have a look at your papers.'

The old man fumbled inside his coat. He brought out two cards. Valremy looked at both of them. They said, André Martin, French, aged fifty-three. The second card also said 'War wounded' at the top. Valremy looked at the photos on the two cards. Then he looked up. 'Take off your beret,' he said.

The man took it off. Valremy checked the photos with the man in front of him. It was the same face. The man in front of him looked ill. He had cut himself shaving, and small bits of toilet paper were stuck on the cuts. His face was grey and greasy with sweat.

'What do you want to go down there for?'

'I live there,' said the old man. 'In an attic. I'm on a pension.'

Valremy looked at the address on the cards. It was 154 Rue de Rennes. The CRS man looked at the house above his head. It was number 132. So number 154 must be further down the road. No orders against letting an old man go home, he thought.

'All right. Pass through. But don't get into any trouble. The President is going to be along in a couple of hours.'

The old man smiled, putting his cards away. He nearly

stumbled on his one leg and crutch. Valremy reached out to steady him.

'I know,' the old man said. 'One of my mates is getting his medal. I got mine two years ago.' He tapped the Freedom medal on his coat.

He hobbled away down the street. The CRS man turned to stop another person trying to slip through the barrier. 'All right. All right. That's enough of that. Stay back behind the barrier.'

The last thing he saw of the old soldier was the tail of the greatcoat as he went into a doorway at the far end of the street, near the square.

Bertha looked up from her knitting as the shadow fell over her. It had been a tiring day, what with all those policemen looking in all the rooms.

'Excuse me, madam. I was wondering . . . maybe a glass of water. It is so hot waiting for the President to come.'

She took in the face and form of an old man in a greatcoat. It was like the one her husband used to wear years ago. He leaned heavily on a crutch, only one leg showing under the greatcoat. His face looked drawn and ill.

'Oh, you poor man. Walking around like that, and in this heat. The President doesn't come for two hours yet. You are early. Come on in.'

She shuffled off to the glass-fronted door of her room at the back of the hall. The old soldier hobbled after her.

She took a glass and turned on the tap. Above the running of the water she did not hear the outer door close. She hardly felt the man's left hand slide round her neck from behind. The crash of his fist on the bone on the side of her head came as a shock. The sight of the running water and the glass in front of her burst into flashes of red and black. Her limp body slid to the floor.

6 Lebel's last chance

The Jackal opened the front of his coat. He undid the strap that had kept his right leg bent up. He winced with pain as the blood flowed back into his lower leg.

Five minutes later Bertha was bound up hand and foot with her own washing line. Her mouth was covered with a large piece of sticking plaster. He put her in the kitchen and shut the door.

He found the keys of the flats in a drawer. He picked up the crutch and looked outside. The hall was empty. He locked the kitchen door after him and went upstairs.

He chose a flat on the sixth floor and knocked. There was no sound. He knocked at the flat next door. No sound from there either. He found the right key and went into the first flat. He locked the door after him.

He crossed to the window and looked out. On the roof-tops across the road, men in blue uniforms were taking up their posts. He was only just in time. He undid the window catch and swung both halves quietly inwards into the room.

Stepping to the side of the window, he found he could look downwards and sideways into the station yard. It was 130 metres away. He moved the living room table until it was eight feet back from the window and well to one side. He took off the cloth and put two cushions on it to form his firing rest.

He took off his overcoat and rolled up his sleeves. Then he took the crutch apart, piece by piece. He took off the black rubber cap from the bottom piece of the crutch. Inside were his last three last shells. The sick feeling brought on by eating the cordite from the other two was only just wearing off.

From another part of the crutch he drew out the silencer; from another part the telescopic sight. Next came the breech and the barrel. The padded armpit rest had the trigger hidden inside it. When he had taken out the trigger, the padded rest slid on to the stock of the gun to be held against the shoulder.

He put the parts of the rifle together carefully. He sat on a chair behind the table and rested the barrel of the gun on top of the cushions. He looked through the telescopic sight. The head of one of the men in the station yard passed across the line of sight. The head looked large and clear, as large as the melon had in the forest.

He lined the three bullets up on the edge of the table. With finger and thumb he slid back the bolt of the rifle and put the first bullet into the breech. One should be enough, but he had two spare. He pushed the bolt until it closed on the base of the bullet, gave a half-twist, and locked it. Then he laid the rifle gently on the table and got out his cigarettes. He lit up and leant back. He had more than an hour and a half to wait.

For the first time in many years, Lebel was really frightened. His mouth felt dry with fear. He was sure that something was going to happen that afternoon, and he still had no clues as to how or when.

He walked slowly among the crowds at the barriers. The people were so far back from the station yard that no one could see what was going on. Each policeman he spoke to told him the same thing. No one had passed through the barriers since they went up at noon.

The main roads were blocked; the side roads were blocked; the alleys were blocked. The roof-tops were being watched and guarded. The station itself was crawling with policemen. They sat on top of the engine sheds, high above the silent platforms. All trains had been moved to another station for that afternoon. Every building near by had been searched.

Lebel slipped through the side streets, showing his police pass. He took a short cut to the Rue de Rennes. It was the same story. The road was blocked off, empty but for CRS men on patrol. He started asking again.

'Seen anyone?'

'No, sir.'

'Anyone been past – anyone at all?'

'No, sir.'

Down in the station yard he could hear the band tuning up. He looked at his watch. The President would be coming any time now.

'Seen anyone pass?'

'No, sir, not this way.'

'All right. Carry on.'

Down in the square he heard an order shouted. A motorcade drove into the square. He saw it turn into the gates of the station yard, police at the salute. All eyes in the crowds were on the sleek, black cars. He looked up at the roof-tops. Good boys. The watchers there kept *their* eyes on the roof-tops and windows across the road.

He had reached the western side of the Rue de Rennes. A young CRS man stood with his feet planted firmly apart at the barrier. He was guarding the gap where the last steel barrier came up to the wall of number 132.

'Anybody passed this way?'

'No, sir?'

'How long have you been here?'

'Since noon when the street was closed.'

'Nobody been through that gap?'

'No, sir. Well, only the old cripple, and he lives down there.'

'What cripple?' Lebel asked him.

'Oldish chap. Looked sick as a dog. He had his papers. "War wounded" they said. Address, 154 Rue de Rennes. Well, I had to let *him* through. He looked all in. Not surprised with him in that Army greatcoat, and in this heat. Daft, I call it.'

'Greatcoat?'

'Yes, sir. Long Army greatcoat, like the old soldiers used to wear. Too hot for a day like this, though.'

'You said he was war wounded. What was wrong with him?'

'Only one leg, sir. Hobbling along, he was. On a crutch.'

'Crutch?' Lebel's voice sounded far away.

'Yes, sir. A crutch, like men with one leg always have. A metal crutch.'

Lebel was racing off down the street, yelling at the CRS man to follow him.

In the square the old soldiers were drawn up in the sunlight. The cars were parked nose-to-tail along the station wall. The President's party had formed a group facing the old soldiers. The band started to play.

The Jackal looked down the telescopic sight of the rifle into the station yard. He picked out the old soldier nearest to him, the one who would be the first to get his medal. He was a short, stocky man, standing very straight. His head came clearly into the sight. In a few minutes, another man, about a foot taller, would be standing in front of him – a man with a proud face, large nose and with two gold stars on the front of his uniform hat.

The last notes of the band died away. There was a great silence. The order to the guard rang out, 'Present Arms.' The white-gloved hands moved as one hand across rifle butts, and heels came down together. A single tall form moved forward and walked proudly to the line of old soldiers. The rest of the staff stayed back. Only the War Minister who would present the old soldiers to their President came forward with him. Slightly behind then walked a man with a velvet cushion. On it were pinned ten medals.

'This one?' Lebel stopped, out of breath. He pointed to a doorway.

'I think so, sir. Yes, this was it. Next to the end one. This was where he went in,' the CRS man said.

The little detective was gone down the hallway and the CRS man followed him. When Valremy got into the hall, Lebel was shaking the door of the caretaker's room. There was no sound from inside. Lebel smashed the frosted glass panel with his elbow, reached inside and opened the door.

'Follow me,' he called and dashed inside.

'Too right, I'm going to follow you,' the CRS man thought. 'You're off your head.'

He found Lebel at the door of the kitchen. Looking over the

man's shoulder he saw Bertha, the caretaker, tied up on the floor. 'Blimey,' Valremy said. Suddenly he realized the little man was not playing games. They *were* after a criminal. This was the big moment he had always dreamed of, and he wished he was back at the barracks.

'Top floor,' shouted Lebel. Valremy ran after him, getting out his gun as he went.

7   Now!

The President of France stopped in front of the first old soldier. He bent down a little to listen to the Minister who was telling him who the old soldier was. Then the President turned to the man with the cushion and took a medal. As the band began to play softly, the President pinned the medal on to the chest of the proud old man in front of him. Then he stepped back for the salute.

130 metres away and six floors up the Jackal held the rifle very steady. He peered down the sight. He could see the face quite clearly: the peak of the hat, the large nose. He saw the hand raised in salute come down from the hat. The crossed wires of the telescopic sight were spot on the temple. Softly, gently, he pulled the trigger.

A split second later he was staring down into the station yard. He could not believe his eyes. Before the bullet had passed out of the gun the President had bent his head down without warning. As the Jackal watched, stunned, he kissed the old soldier on each cheek. To do so, he had had to bend down, as he was a good foot taller than the old soldier. It is a French custom for one man to greet another with a kiss on each cheek. The Jackal, being English, had not thought of this.

Later it was found that the bullet had passed less than a quarter of an inch behind the moving head. The President gave no sign that he heard it. Nor did anyone else. The bullet tore into the tarmac which was soft from the heat. The band played on. The President stood up straight and moved slowly on to the next man.

Behind his gun, the Jackal started to swear with anger, but softly. He had never missed a standing target at 150 yards in his life. Then he calmed down. There was still time. He tore open the breech of the rifle and put in another bullet.

Lebel reached the sixth floor. His heart was beating so fast it felt as though it would tear his chest apart. There were two doors leading to the front of the block. He looked from one to the other as the CRS man caught up with him. From behind one of the doors came a low, but clear, 'phut' noise. Lebel pointed at the door lock.

'Shoot it off,' he whispered, and stepped back. The CRS man braced himself on both feet and fired. Bits of wood and metal flew everywhere. The door swung inwards. Valremy was first into the room, Lebel on his heels.

The CRS man could see the grey tufts of hair of the old soldier, but that was all. The man had two legs, the greatcoat was gone, and the hands that gripped the rifle were young and strong. The gunman gave him no time. Jumping up from the table, he fired from the hip. The bullet made hardly a sound. It tore into Valremy's chest and exploded. He felt only great ripping, stabs of pain. Then even they were gone and it was all dark.

Above his body, Lebel stared into the eyes of the gunman.

'Jackal,' he said.

The other man simply said, 'Lebel.' He was doing something to his gun. Lebel saw a spent shell case drop to the floor. The gunman took something off the table and put it into the breech. His cold, grey eyes were still staring at Lebel.

'He's trying to stare me out,' thought Lebel. 'He is going to kill me.'

With an effort he dropped his eyes from the gunman's gaze. Valremy's submachine-gun lay at his feet. Without thinking, he dropped to his knees and grabbed the gun, swinging it upwards with one hand. The other hand felt for the trigger. He heard the Jackal snap home the breech of the rifle. Lebel found the trigger of the submachine-gun and pulled it.

Half a magazine-full of bullets hit the Jackal in the chest, picked him up, half-turned him in the air, and slammed his body into a heap in the corner of the room.

Superintendent Thomas had a phone call from Paris that evening. He was told, 'We have got him. No problems, but you had better get up to his flat and sort things out.'

'It was eight o'clock by the time the inspector had sorted through the last of Calthrop's belongings. Suddenly, he heard a sound at the open doorway. He turned round. A man was standing there, staring at him.

'Who are you?' Thomas asked him.

'Charles Calthrop, and this is my flat. What the hell are you doing here?'

'All right,' Thomas said quietly. 'I think you had better come down to Scotland Yard for a little chat.'

They held him at the Yard for twenty-four hours – until they had proof from France that the Jackal was dead. They held him still – until the landlords of five inns in the north of Scotland had all told the police that Charles Calthrop had indeed spent the last three weeks touring Scotland.

'If the Jackal wasn't Calthrop,' said Thomas to the police chief at Scotland Yard, 'then who the hell was he?'

The police chief said, 'The British Government cannot admit that he was an Englishman at all. A certain Englishman was suspect for a time. He has now been cleared. We know that the Jackal posed as an Englishman for a time. But he also passed himself off as a Danish parson, an American student, and a Frenchman. All we can say is that the case is now closed.'

The next day the body of a man was buried in an unmarked grave in a small Paris graveyard. The death certificate showed him as a tourist from abroad, killed on 25 August 1963 in a road crash. The name was not known. A priest, a policeman and two grave-diggers were present. There was one other person there – a little man who would not give his name.

When it was all over, the little man turned and walked out of the graveyard to go back home to his wife.

The day of the Jackal was over.